*S*ave *U*ganda *M*ovement [SUM]

'My Role In Removing Idi Amin'- Copyright © 2014 Paul Opobo Oryema.

All rights reserved. This book or any portion thereof may not be reproduced or used in any manner whatsoever without the express written permission of the publisher except for the use of brief quotations in a book review.

Book ISBN 978-0-9929462-3-4

Publisher:
Alawi Books ltd
125 Second Avenue
Manor Park
London E126EN

Website at:
www.tboah.com

Contacts:
email: info@tboah.com
tel: [+44] 07983412790

Ordering information:

'My Role In Removing Idi Amin' is available as a hard copy from Amazon Book website.

Cover design, Layout and Illustrations: Jack Stevens Alecho-oita
Published by Alawi Books Ltd.
125 Second Avenue, Manor Park, London, E12 6EN.
Copyright©Alawi Books Ltd. 2014.

Contents

ABREVIATIONS 3
DEDICATION 4
THANKS 5
FOREWORD 6
INTRODUCTION 13
1. HERE I COME 14
2. THE PERILOUS POLITICAL ATMOSPHERE 21
3. HEARING THE GOOD NEWS 25
4. OUR TRAINING 32
5. VISITS OF OUR TRAINING CAMP 36
6. FERRYING AND RECEIVING THE 'BLACK MARKET' GOODS 45
7. IN THE OPEN MOUTH OF THE CROCODILE 51
8. THE D-Day AND ITS EFFECT 53
9. TOWARDS THE FALL OF IDI AMIN-DADA's REGIME 61

APPENDICES: 70
    NOTES: 1-18 70
    Afterword - 1: HOW HAS THE MIGHTY FALLEN? 107
    Afterword - 2: THE AFTERMATH 128
    Afterword - 3: RUMINATION 144
    Afterword - 4: I PROTEST 149

FLAGPOSTS: 181
1. Save Uganda Movement – Special Forces deployed during the 1978/1978 Liberation War against Idi Amin-Dada 181
2. Map of Uganda – spread/origin of SUM special forces 184
3. SUM Operational Epi-centres 1977-1979 185
4. SUM Operational Theatres 1978-1979 186
5. AKENA p'OJOK 187

Epilogue 188
Subject Index 191
    My wandering Profile - Author 200

Save Uganda Movement [SUM]

ABREVIATIONS

SUM	-	Save Uganda Movement
NDG	-	Nairobi Discussion Group
UNM	-	Uganda National Movement
TPDF	-	Tanzania Peoples Defence Force
UNLF	-	Uganda National Liberation Front
UNLA		Uganda National Liberation Army
NCC	-	National Consultative Council
MC	-	Military Commission
KM	-	Kikos Maalum
KiMi	-	Kitgum Militia
FRONASA	-	Front for National Salvation
PFLU	-	Popular Front for the Liberation of Uganda
SRB	-	State Research Bureau
GSU	-	General Service Unit
UPC	-	Uganda Peoples Congress
DP	-	Democratic Party
RPF	-	Rwanda Patriotic Front
KAR	-	Kings African Rifles
NRA	-	National Resistance Army
NRM	-	National Resistance Movement
LRA	-	Lord's Resistance Army
UPDF	-	Uganda Peoples Defence Force

DEDICATION

This is dedicated to Mwalimu Julius Kambarage Nyerere[1], former President of the United Republic of Tanzania; one of the greatest sons of Africa that has ever lived, who could see clearly the plight of the oppressed Ugandans during Idi Amin-Dada's tyrannical rule and did something about it.

It also dedicated to **S**ave **U**ganda **M**ovement (SUM) combatants who paid the ultimate price to free Uganda from the tyrannical rule of Idi Amin-Dada Dada: namely[2] Mr David Kitara, Mr Charles Oburu, Mr Gulu, Mr Okech Ojukwu, Mr Benjamin Ojok and Mr John Okumu Samora. Your precious blood made it possible for Ugandans to regain their freedom from the hands of the tyrant.

May your soul rest in eternal peace till we meet again.

Paul Opobo Oryema

---

[1] Was recalled by his ancestors on 14 October 1999; and now rested at Butiama in Tanzania.

[2] See details of all named here in Flagposts 1 & 2

Save Uganda Movement [SUM]

THANKS

A special thanks goes to Flight Engineer Jack Oita Alecho who urged me to tell our story otherwise no one will tell it without distortion. Eng. Oita sent me the money which enabled me to gather all the information needed for writing our story.

Special thanks also go to Fredrick Olobo Agwa[3] who assisted me in every way possible to write and send the scripts for publication in London, United Kingdom.

Paul Opobo Oryema

---

[3] First born and son to the Late Jacob Okello-Agwa (JAO) [RIP].
** JAO was one of the central drivers to the ending of Idi Amin-Dada's governance since 1971; in 1973 was key to the formation of Save Uganda Movement (SUM). From 1979 Post-Idi Amin, JAO served in various civil service positions and was appointed by the Yoweri Kaguta Museveni's NRA-regime as Uganda Ambassador to the Democratic Republic of Congo (DRC) but never effected.
*** JAO was recalled by his ancestors in 2012 and is now rested at Amuru.

FOREWORD

SAVE UGANDA MOVEMENT [S.U.M].

Save Uganda Movement (SUM) came into existence in the later part of 1972, after the fiasco of attack, by Ugandan exiles, on Idi Amin-Dada's Masada and Mbarara barracks in September 1972. It was founded by a group of young men and women both within and without Uganda. There were young politician/nationalists, professionals (Doctors, Engineers, etc.), soldiers and policemen and ordinary non-denominational and common men. SUM members were of all political parties, religions and ethnic groups and had one AIM in common: To remove Idi Amin-Dada from power by any means possible. It built an elaborate net-worked information system to collect and inform outside world of Idi Amin-Dada's atrocities, misinform and dis-inform Idi Amin-Dada and often pre-emptied and saved lives of would be victims of brutal murders. It thoroughly infiltrated Idi Amin-Dada's Airforce and Telecommunications systems and had informers among close escorts and bodyguards.

SUM operated from Nairobi, Busia, Jinja, Entebbe, Kampala and Kitgum; with contacts in Gulu, Soroti, Arusha, Dar es Salaam and London. Its recruitment of members was personal and individual contacts; and its operations were strictly clandestine. It became overtly action-orientated between 1974-75 that successfully bombed Kampala and Jinja; and disrupted electricity supplies, oil dumps, Railway and Military vehicles. The intention was to bring to the attention of the world, and particularly the Organisation of African Unity (OAU), the plight of the Ugandan people under Idi Amin-Dada. It was hoped Idi Amin-Dada would be forced to postpone the scheduled OAU meeting the May of 1975. (It is on record that only a few Heads of State attended that conference and many of the few hurried away a few hours later, the same day or over-night).

Idi Amin-Dada was exposed as never before. This made him angry.

Subsequent actions and events such as the harassment of Idi Amin-Dada himself (ambushes), causing misunderstanding between officers of the Army and those of **S**tate **R**esearch **B**ureau (SRB)[4], leaking of secret documents and plans to the press etc., angered Idi Amin-Dada inexorably. The more he was angry, the more he behaved stupidly, albeit atrociously, and his very existence became vulnerable. SUM finally came to dictate its overt actions from March 1978 up to the conclusion of the Liberation war, in 1979. Idi Amin-dada ordered an attack on Tanzania in September 1978; what this led to, we all now know.

Tanzania is a stable country with stable institutions. Because it was in logger-heads with Idi Amin-Dada, it had to deploy its intelligence to know more about Uganda in general and the activities of the political exiles in particular. The speed per excellence Tanzania therefore; on political conclusions, Moshi Unity Conference and execution of the Liberation war was a testimony of their spot-on insight of, knowledge of and working with Ugandan exiles.

On the political front SUM initiated and organised the "**N**airobi **D**iscussion **G**roup" (NDG) which became the geographical and academic focal-point for the liberation of Uganda. The NDG organised or facilitated meetings of the, and between various anti-Amin factions, including conferences/meetings held in Nairobi, Arusha, Dar es Salaam, Lusaka [Uganda National Movement (UNM)], London and New York. It established strong links with anti-Amin lobbies in these capitals. The Moshi Conference of March 1979 was the brain child of members of the NDG, and principally the Uganda National Liberation Front

---

[4] Bonafide State security intelligence under the Idi Amin-Dada regime.

(UNLF) documents were adopted directly from the NDG work papers. The UNLF's National Consultative Council (NCC) drew together largest single group of some of the best brains Uganda had at the time, for the first time. This is because of horizontal-linkage system SUM was operating throughout the world.

If **S**ave **U**ganda **M**ovement (SUM) could not claim its humble contributions to the liberation of Uganda by "...*baiting Idi Amin-Dada to the snares*...", it could at least claim the provision of first class intelligence information on Idi Amin-Dada's military equipment and armaments, Army units deployment, etc., etc., and liberation of large sections of the East and North East of Uganda, including the whole of Kitgum District, - before the main Tanzania Peoples Defence Force (TPDF)-led Liberation Forces arrived in the area.

SUM was not a political party and there was no intention of making it one. It was a national movement to carry out a specific job. Its members faithfully abided by its rules and regulations. After the job was completed its members fell back to whatever political parties or groups they had belonged to.

1979[5].

The liberation forces advance to the North and East of Kampala was delayed for the combination of the following reasons: -

1. Tanzania Peoples Defence Forces (TPDF) wanted to rest its army and re-organise logistics in Kampala before the push - to the - North could proceed on the central axis and eastern axis. But the army "over-rested". The soldiers were lured into and begun to find the comfort of excessive Kampala hospitality - drinks and women. The Kikosi Maalum (KM)[6] too indulged in excessive drinks, petty

---

[5] References to "*War in Uganda - The Legacy of Idi Amin*", by Tony Avirgan and Martha Honey)

[6] Designated military arm of the Tanzania Peoples Defence Force (TPDF) of Ugandans fighting alongside Tanzanians in the 1978-79 war between

thefts, looting, and hunting down individual suspected Idi Amin-Dada-men with a view to revenge and to appropriate their property. It became extremely difficult to keep the soldiers and some TPDF officers to mind the war.

2. President Yusuf Kironde-Lule himself was no longer interested in the war - (could not even imagine that Idi Amin-Dada could make a comeback if left intact!) Some of his remarks earned him disfavour with the TPDF and suspicion from the KM - some of these factors cost him his Presidency - in only 68 days. Kironde-Lule was as blind as a bat to political factors of the war; to him to-be-liberated Uganda border stopped at Jinja 50 miles east, and Nakasongola 70 miles north of Kampala.

3. But more importantly was the question of securing the Owen Falls Power Station (OFPS) and Dam without damage from Idi Amin-Dada's soldiers. Meanwhile Idi Amin-Dada had announced through a pirate radio that his last strong foothold would be in Jinja and that he would fight "...*to the death...*" here. Both military and civilian intelligence reported that Jinja was indeed garrisoned and Idi Amin-Dada - soldiers have dug-in everywhere, their artillery placements faced strategic points in the Western bank, including the OFPS. Rumours also had it that both road and the railway bridges were heavily mined and that the dam itself and the power station were rigged with tons of high explosives. As Minister of Energy, and as one who had worked in and knew the OFPS and the vicinity well and also as one who was actively participating in the liberation efforts through an under-cover clandestine organisation '...*Save Uganda Movement (SUM)*...', I was approached by the TPDF top brass for information and suggestions, if any.

Tanzania and Uganda. A war that eventually got rid of Idi Amin-Dada's regime.

We compared notes and available information. The TPDF were conspicuously concerned about crossing the Nile. The alternative proposal that 2 brigades proceed to the North crossing the Nile at Karuma Bridge, and then to the East, then attack Idi Amin-Dada's soldiers from the back, were abandoned. It was correctly reasoned that if all retreat routes were cut-off, it would force Idi Amin-Dada and the bulk of his trusted soldiers, indeed, to fight "...to the death..."

I still knew practically every Uganda Electricity Board (UEB) staff in the power station, and I kept telephone contacts with them. I had earlier ordered that essential operations staff must remain in the station, be supplied with 14-days foodstuff and should continue to generate electricity as long as possible. I was reliably informed by several of them and by SUM that it was not true that the Power Station, the damn and the railway bridge had been rigged up with explosives, and that even Idi Amin-Dada's men were not in the Power Station building itself. Despite these assurances I gave to the TPDF that in fact there were no high explosives or mines on the Dam, Bridge or Railway Bridge there was reluctance to believe and use the UEB report. In any case the problem of Idi Amin-Dada's menacing artillery on the eastern bank facing west and aimed at every approach to the Nile was still not resolved. A difficult decision had to be made within 24 hours. At the same time, the ideas of storming of the Jinja Western bank by crack troops crossing the Nile under cover of darkness over the road and Railway bridges and by boat were rejected as being too risky, as there were likely to result in a large number of causalities. At the same time (it should be remembered that President Julius Nyerere was determined to fight a tactical political war; he controlled his army with iron-fist; he always checked and agreed to a next phase of attack only if he was convinced that losses on both sides shall be minimal.

I called the SUM caucus to action. We agreed on a deception-tactics, a method used earlier on in make believe BBC broadcast

> "...that the liberation forces have in-fact, already infiltrated the Jinja area including a crack commando unit of the TPDF which was holding the Owen Falls Power Station (OFPS) itself...";

and it should be let:
- known to Idi Amin-Dada and his soldiers that Jinja and environ has in fact already been infiltrated;
- and reactivate the SUM "...*boys*..." acting under cover in the area to provide the desired audio and visual effect to this deception.

For access to British Broadcasting Corporation (BBC) broadcast we decided to use the services of Mr Richard Posnett, the British Ag. High Commissioner (1979-80), who was seeing me twice a day to collect "...*the latest news*..." SUM "...*boys*..." in Jinja who were lying low except for intelligence information gathering were re-activated to active duty. As soon as the BBC broadcast the deception story, SUM moved out, on foot in, in canoes and on bicycles, to strategic positions in town, high grounds, surrounding hills and sugar plantations where they exploded mines, explosives, hand grenades and opened rifle fires in the air. Idi Amin-Dada's Uganda Army (UA) having heard the BBC broadcast coupled with rumour-filled Jinja air and explosives in the night, apparently believed the deception story.

The deception tactics worked.

The next morning, to the total consternation of the residents, the UA began to move, - to withdraw from dug-in positions. What earlier started as an orderly withdrawal, became a stampede. The UA abandoned some of its heavy installed equipment in situ on the East bank. When I passed this information to the TPDF, they were not amused. The TPDF command was already angry at the BBC broadcast and was not prepared to listen to "...*Sci-fi*..." The TPDF protested to the

LULE government - that government must not issue statements on the conduct of the war without "...*mutual*..." consultation and consent. Nevertheless, the TPDF softened their tone, and tension abated, especially as their own military intelligence started reporting the UA withdrawal as well. A few days later, it was reported that Jinja was now secured more or less intact, and no damage was done to the OFPS. The TPDF lavished the "...*civilians*..." of Jinja with praise and thanks for their contribution to the war effort.

AKENA p'OJOK.

INTRODUCTION

This book highlights the insight role of Save Uganda Movement (SUM) in the ending and removal of the Idi Amin-Dada military regime in Uganda. As the author, and SUM guerrilla commander the records I am sharing here are from the position I was standing, and therefore unlikely to have the full pictures of what other drivers held by the SUM political leaders were helpful in this endeavour. This is in keeping with 'Need to Know' modus operandi, which made it possible for the Tanzania political leadership and military command to trust the SUM from conception to a successful execution of all the operations inside the enemy territory.

Chapters 1 to 8 signposts the readers to the humble origin, the process and conclusions of my role as a guerrilla commander. I have laid it out this way so that the readers are taken through the immediate steps that effected the removing of the Idi Amin-Dada military regime.

Appended Notes 1 to 18 offers readers more appropriate insights in terms of reviews, opinions and analysis of various phases of the struggle to end Idi Amin-Dada's military rule. The Afterword 1 to 4 captures a few of my afterthoughts and learning from the consequences of my action in particular, and SUM in general.

Flagposts offers readers pictorials of the SUM operational epicentres and theatres that are variously mentioned in this book.

1.

HERE I COME

I am Paulo Opobo Oryema. I am from Keyo, Palema Parish, Lamogi sub-county, Kilak County, Amur District.

On 8th April 1948 I was born by noon to Mr Minayo Oryema and Ms Magdalena Apoko.

My mother told me that she was alone at home that day when I ventured into the world; other folks had gone to tend to their crops in the field, when labour pains began, she went behind our hut where she endured birth pain until I was born. Having had a successful delivery, she then cut off the umbilical cord and we moved in the hut.

When other folks returned home from the field, it was all wonder and joy to find me crying in the hut. All wondered how my mother managed this feat without the help of any village midwife.

I was the fifth child in the family of nine children, with four boys and five girls. Our first born was John Okoya, followed by Geraldine Auma, Martina Anek, Obal who passed on when he was still a toddler, me, Oyella, Helen Amony, Rose Akidi and Christine Aryemo.

I am from Lamogi clan of the central Luo (Acoli). It suffices to recall the Lamogi Rebellion of 1911-12 when my ancestors rebelled against the British colonial rule. To quote: '*...Then major cause of this rebellion was the demand by British colonialists to have guns owned by Acholi people registered so that unwanted use of guns is prevented, a factor which didn't go*

well with the populace hence sparking off the fight[7]...'
Rebellion therefore is something which is in my blood. I love freedom because right from childhood my father brought me up never to accept to become someone's slave. Should any of my siblings fail to do something up to his expectation, he would retort by saying that such one was destined to be a slave. My involvement in rebellion against Idi Amin-Dada's' regime was a matter of course.

My father was a liberal person. He did not insist on seeing to it that all his children should become Protestants like him. As a consequence, some of my siblings became Catholics like my mother. My father taught me how to read and write the Luo alphabet and numbers. Once I had mastered these, he then sent me to Keyo Primary School where I began P1 (Primary One) in 1957.

When I began going to school our home was about four kilometres away from school. I used to endure dew on the path to school such that my school uniform especially the pair of shorts could not last long enough until the end of each year. To overcome this state of affair, my father was forced to move our home near to the school. This helped me a great deal from arriving at school each morning when my school uniform was partly wet.

I pursued my primary education at Keyo Primary school up to P6 (Primary Six) and sat for the Primary Leaving Examination (PLE). I passed the examination in a high second grade and proceeded to Agole Junior Secondary School at Pabbo in 1962. Pabbo is about 45kms from Keyo, along the Juba Highway. When I completed J1 (Junior One), I was unable to proceed to J2 (Junior Two) due to lack of money for school fees. I stayed at home from 1963 up to 1965 due to this.

---

[7]   See briefing link: http://www.pmldaily.com/news/2017/12/lamogi-rebellion-guru-guru-hill-named-tourist-site.html

I went back to Junior Secondary School in 1966 when my late elder brother Mr John Okoya took me to Kampala where he was working. While in Kampala, I attended my J2 (Junior Two) at Namanve Education Institute, Bweyogerere. I attained Grade One in the 1966 Junior Leaving Examination and proceeded the following year to Kitante Hill Senior Secondary School, that is S1 (senior one) to S4 (senior four). I completed my 'O' Level education there in 1970 have attained Grade One Certificate. I then proceeded to Old Kampala Senior Secondary School for my H1 (higher one) and H2 (higher 2) for the 'A' Level education where I did **P**hysics/**C**hemistry/**M**athematics [PCM] combination. Old Kampala Senior Secondary School then was one of the Asian schools in Kampala. Teachers in that school were predominantly Asians and Whites. The expulsion of Asians from Uganda by Idi Amin-Dada in 1972 affected so much the performance of students in the 1972 'O' & 'A' Level Examinations. As a consequence, my performance in the 1972 'A' Level Examination was not good enough to see me to Makerere University.

Later in 1974, I joined the National Teachers College Kyambogo, where I trained as a secondary school teacher. I completed the course in 1976 with a Diploma in Education. My teaching subjects were Mathematics and French. After a successful completion of my teaching practice, I was posted to Kololo Senior Secondary School as a teacher.

At the end of June 1974, thanks to the benevolence of the French government we student teachers from **National Teachers College [NTC] Kyambogo**, and Makerere University were offered scholarships to France.

> On 30th June 1976, we proceeded to France for our language bath.

We left that day Entebbe Airport in a tense mood because;

> On 27th June an Air France plane was hijacked by Palestinian guerrillas and brought to Entebbe Airport.

Then Idi Amin-Dada pretended to handle the negotiation for release of Israelis who were passengers of the plane.

We reached France safely at Orly Airport in Paris in an Air France flight. We then proceeded by train to Vichy where CAVILAM[8] is situated. It was at CAVILAM where we had our language bath for six months. French teachers from Makerere University had their language bath for only three months and returned back to Uganda.

On 4th July, I went for prayer service at a French Reformed Church with some of my colleagues.

At the end of the prayer service, the conducting priest greeted all those who attended. He then greeted us again as we were leaving the church, at the same time, asked us where we came from. We told him that we came from Uganda. He then told us that Israeli commandos raided Entebbe Airport and freed the 100 hostages on the Air France plane the previous night. We thanked God for setting free his people.

Two of my colleagues were Rwandese refugees of Tutsi[9] origin. They were Mr Titus Rutaremara and Mr Charles Matsiko. At the end of our language bath Mr Titus Rutaremara did not come back with us to Uganda, he proceeded to Belgium where he went on pursuing further studies. Mr Charles Matsiko came back to Uganda but later on went to Kenya as an economic refugee. I last heard of him teaching French in a Kenyan School at Mombasa. As fate would have it all these college mates of mine became leaders of Rwanda Patriotic Front [RPF][10]. I met Mr Titus Rutaremara on Jinja Road in Kampala after RPF had already taken over power in Rwanda from President Juvenal Habyalimana[11].

---

[8] https://www.cavilam.com/en/the-school/
[9] A historical factor to this involved ethnic conflict/domination of Rwanda by the Hutu.
[10] Formed 1987 in Uganda by refugees of Tutsi origin who went on to seize political control of Rwanda from the Hutu in 1994; Ibid 8.

He told me that he had already attained a PhD and had written a book.

Going back to France, as we settled down in our language bath, we found ourselves among foreign students almost from all over the world. Idi Amin-Dada's name was foul then and we had no pride of being Ugandans because of this. In the course of our interactions with foreign students, some would at times ask us some unpalatable questions about our President. Some would ask whether Idi Amin-Dada was insane or whether he was a cannibal. We would only politely answer by stating that it was only Idi Amin-Dada who could answer such questions to the satisfaction of any inquiring mind.

Despite such derogatory attitude on the part of some foreign students about Idi Amin-Dada, we did our best to show the world what Uganda is by showing the rich culture we have. During cultural evenings organised by the Institute, we managed to stage Uganda traditional songs and dances to their delight.

However, foreign students from progressive countries of the world demonstrated most of the time a spirit of sympathy with the Ugandan situation then, whenever we interacted with them. They advised us in strict confidence to do something about Idi Amin-Dada if Uganda was to gain back its dignity and pride. Some of us took note of their opinion with a lot of thanks.

But a remark by one Nigerian girl about her perception of Ugandan men shocked me to the core. I cannot recall how this came about. All the same she told me point blank that we Ugandan men behave as women. They find us too soft. We are not manly enough. May be that was why Idi Amin-Dada was doing whatever he fancied with us. We were not manly enough to stand up against some of his excesses. Prove to Idi Amin-Dada that you too are men, that is, when he will come to his senses. The remark of this Nigerian girl hit me so low, but the onus was

---

[11] Killed in a plane crash on '...*6th April 1994*...'; Ibid 8&9

on us Ugandan men to prove that we were men like Idi Amin-Dada not women. Point noted!

Our language bath at CAVILAM proceeded very well. We met Frenchmen from several walks of life, at their various work places. We were at times invited for lunch by French families to enable us to get to know better French culture apart from normal lessons from the Institute. We would at times go for excursions, whereby we visited historical sites.

After six months of language bath, we returned to Uganda in January 1977. I then resumed teaching at Kololo Senior Secondary School. But I had hardly settled into this when another of Idi Amin-Dada's pogrom was on against people of Acholi and Lango origin in particular; and, the Uganda Peoples Congress[12] (UPC) members generally.

> On 10th February 1977, this pogrom started when, a pastoral letter was written by Bishops of Church of Uganda protesting harassments of the church leadership and Christians in general accusing Uganda Armed Forces of atrocities.
>
> On the 16th of the same month, Idi Amin-Dada addressed religious leaders and diplomats at Kampala International Conference Centre (KICC).

Later on that day, the Anglican Archbishop Janani Jakaliya Luwum[13], Ministers Mr Erinayo Oryema[14] and Mr Oboth-Ofumbi[15] were murdered in cold blood by Idi Amin-Dada's State Research Bureau[16] (SRB) personnel. They were accused of involvement in

---

[12] Was the governing political party that was overthrown by the military under Idi Amin-Dada.
[13] Janani Jakaliya Luwum was the Archbishop of the Church of Uganda from 1974 to 1977.
[14] Then Minister of Internal Affairs; also served as Inspector General of Police.
[15] Then Minister of Defence; and before was the Permanent Secretary in the same Ministry of Defence.
[16] Ibid 4.

organising a coup d'état against Idi Amin-Dada's regime. Members of the Centenary Committee of Church of Uganda (CCCU) which was preparing the Church of Uganda's 100th Anniversary were accused of importing arms to overthrow the Idi Amin-Dada's government.

As a norm, the usual characteristics of Idi Amin-Dada's pogrom was purging of officers and other ranks and files in the Uganda Armed Forces of Acholi and Lango origin. There was therefore no exception to this one. The security situation because so hopeless for some of us who happened to come from Acholi and Lango. No one would tell for certain when and where it would all end. One time, Idi Amin-Dada announced an attempted coup against him, and consequent death of many people. I heard of some of my relatives and friends who were members of the Uganda Armed Forces were murdered, and some who escaped from various barracks. Amnesty International's (AI)[17] then estimate was that some 50,000-300,000 Ugandans had been killed by Idi Amin-Dada's regime since January 1971 when he attained power.

---

[17] https://www.amnesty.org/download/Documents/204000/afr590071978en.pdf

2.

THE PERILOUS POLITICAL ATMOSPHERE

The February 1977 pogrom of Idi Amin-Dada against Acholi, Langi and the Uganda Peoples Congress (UPC) members generally hit us most adversity. With my colleagues, we began to debate about what course of action to take to avoid the impending peril that awaited us. We resolved that the best course of action to take was to stay alive at all costs. This we could best do by fleeing the country and come back when peace and security will be there for all Ugandans without any discrimination whatsoever would be there.

This was a bitter decision to arrive at, but we had no choice since we had no guarantee to ensure our existence in Uganda during the Idi Amin-Dada regime. We, of Acholi and Langi origin, were endangered species under this regime. Our elites were subject to progressive elimination whenever it was deemed expedient. As it were, even those who were serving in the Uganda Armed Forces were too subject of elimination. Yet these were development pillars in their respective extended families such as sending their siblings to school. We used to wonder how much they were investing in total annually to this effect. Their investment was on the development of human resources at the expense of investing in property or other tangible assets. No wonder, it was no nowhere then to find modern permanent buildings in Lango and Acholi. The emphasis was in the development of human resources.

In the 1960's, it was a norm in Acholi and Lango for every elite such those who served in the Armed Forces irrespective of their

ranks to take on the educating of children from their extended families, even if one did not have his or her own to educate. It was a matter of pride and competition to do this among them. One was a nonentity if one did not have a child that he or she was sending to school. So, elimination of these development agents was tantamount to causing under development in Acholi and Lango then. Idi Amin-Dada's regime therefore spelt doom for these benevolent endeavours as if it was a crime for them to attain higher education or serve in the Uganda Armed Forces. Most of them were apolitical. They joined the armed forces on merit but not on political grounds. They were patriotic and loyal to Idi Amin-Dada's regime. Since Idi Amin-Dada took power, they had never caused any problem whatsoever to his regime. To the contrary, Idi Amin-Dada was harbouring a lot of fear about their presence in the Uganda Armed Forces. Having committed a lot of atrocities against the Acholi and Langi, Idi Amin-Dada was living in fear of their revenge one day. This was why he took to eliminating them progressively from the Uganda Armed Forces.

Eliminating them from the Uganda Armed Forces was a gross violation of human rights. Acholi and Lango bore the brunt of Idi Amin-Dada's misrule in Uganda. By stating this fact, I am not saying that the other nationalities did not suffer under his misrule. They did suffer too but to a lesser extent.

Idi Amin-Dada's rule right from the onset faced great opposition from within and from without the country. Idi Amin-Dada having even a narrower popular base unleashed such terror and slaughter of Ugandans that Uganda's name in the international community had become inextricably linked with repulsive acts of the dictator.

While the Bill of Rights remained in the institution and the courts of law remained in existence, Uganda suffered the most violent breaches of the rule of law and violation of human rights. In fact right from the beginning of his rule, while some people in Kampala were still celebrating the exit of Dr Apollo Milton Obote[18] as a despot, members of the armed forces who hailed from Lango and Acholi were being crushed to death with military tanks in Jinja, just 50 miles away, and in some other areas. Soldiers and other state security agents notably **State Research Bureau**[19] (SRB) personnel became a special category of people above the law. They could kill, arrest, torture and imprison people with impunity.

The Chief Justice, Mr. Benedicto Kagimu Mugumba Kiwanuka[20], was dragged from his chambers in broad daylight and disappeared. That day when he was arrested people ran in all directions all over and away from Kampala. Eventually, the Anglican Archbishop Jana Luwum, the Vice Chancellor of Makerere University Frank Kalimuzo, Cabinet Ministers[21], Doctors, Clerics, Civil Servants, peasants, even his own wives[22], and their relatives disappeared. The independence of the Judiciary and the rule of law were greatly undermined.

The army in many cases increasingly took over the role of the police in effecting arrests. Disappearances of people became the order of the day. Summary executions by firing squad became common, some of them performed in public. Many people, particularly highly qualified ones sensing danger to their lives, fled to countries which could offer them opportunities to oppose Idi Amin-Dada politically and militarily.

This was the beginning of the popularisation of the armed struggle to resolve political issues though it has to be admitted

---

[18] Was Prime Minister 1961-1965; then President 1965-1971 and again 1980-1985. Was in political exile in Tanzania 1971-1980 and again in Zambia 1985-2006 when he was recalled by the ancestors.

[19] Ibid 4.

[20] While as Chief Justice was murdered in 1973 by the Idi Amin regime. A lawyer by profession and was also the leader of the **Democratic Party** (DP) and Uganda first Chief Minister at the advent of granting Independence from colonial rule.

[21] First causality, then Foreign Minister Lt Col Michael Ondoga was murdered and immediately after being replaced by Princess Elizabeth Bagaya.

[22] First causality was Ms Kay Adroa who was also Mr Michael Ondoga's sister; Ibid 21.

that in Idi Amin-Dada's era there was no other form of struggle possible. This was also the beginning of the movement of large numbers of people, out of the country either as refugees running away from human rights violation or as a result of economic hardship.

The massive expulsion of Asian (many of them Ugandans citizens[23]) from Uganda, in 1972 on racial grounds and the expropriation of their properties did not only expedite the decline of the economy but was also a gross violation of human rights. The subsequent mismanagement of these properties and the economy in general destroyed the industrial, commercial, tourism, and agricultural sectors of the economy. Idi Amin-Dada persecuted some religious sects and in fact banned all of them except the three large sects of the Catholics, Protestants, and the Muslims. He created animosity between religions by favouring the minority Muslims at the expense of the Christians.

---

[23] Idi Amin is variously quoted that in August 1972, gave most of Uganda's 80,000 Asians 90 days to leave.

3.

HEARING THE GOOD NEWS

In February 1977, after the death of Anglican Archbishop Janani Luwum and Ministers Mr Erinayo Wilson Oryema[24] and Mr Alupakusadi Charles Kole Oboth-Ofumbi[25], I went into exile with my three colleagues: Mr Justine Ocitti, Mr Seraphina Oola and Mr Thomas Oringa. Upon reaching Nairobi, we registered with Joint Refugee Service of Kenya [JRSK] as refugees. JRSK gave us accommodation at Trinity College Eastleigh and began giving us a monthly subsistence allowance.

Once in exile every one of us was yearning about what course of action one could take to one's advantage. I wanted to teach in any Secondary School if possible, to pursue further studies. My two colleagues, Mr Ocitti Justine and Mr Seraphina Oola who were graduates from Makerere University wanted to get jobs, or go for their Master's Degrees in their field of specialisation if possible.

As a matter of routine, we used to go to JRSK to meet new arrivals from Uganda or go about exploring Nairobi. We used to go to eat at Shauri Moyo market. There we were meeting Kenyan women of Luo origin who were selling food at the market. Upon knowing that we were Acholi (Luo from Uganda as they would call us), would joke with us that we Luo made a mistake of remaining in Uganda, that we could have followed then up to Kenya. That if we had done so, we would have avoided this kind of misfortune we were facing then in Uganda. We would tell

---

[24] Ibid 14
[25] Ibid 15

them that we had already followed them, better late than never! We would laugh heartily.

It did not take long before other Ugandan refugees who had been in exile since 1971 in Kenya, began visiting us at Trinity College. They welcomed us into exile and educated us about the perils of being in exile. They then asked us as to how long we were prepared to be in exile. We told them that we wished to go back to our country as soon as possible God's willing. They then asked us as to what one would do if an adversary came against one having a Shield and Spear to fight one. We told them that one would take his Shields and Spears to defend himself against the advance of the adversary. They then told us that we answered correctly and told us that there was an opportunity for us to get Shields and Spears for us to go home and face the adversary.

Some of us took notice of what they told us. If we got them right, they were telling us that there was an opportunity for us to go for military training to enable us even scores with Idi Amin-Dada and the system he had created to liberate our country. They then left leaving us with this food for thought.

We began to think about this proposal by weighing its pros and cons. We began selling this proposal in strict confidence. Many rejected the proposal outright. They called those who sold the idea to us '...*self-seekers*...' who wanted to use us to gain power at our expense. Some told us that elites were not supposed to do such a thing, we could contribute at another level should there be a regime change in future in Uganda. Thus, was a typical attitude among Acholi and Lango elites then that they were not to be seen embarking on any armed struggle, it was like the less educated amongst us to do so.

I was of a strong view that all of us irrespective of our level of education should join forces in liberating ourselves from Idi Amin-Dada's tyrannical rule. It was regrettable that our elites had contrary views about it. I would wonder at their myopic attitude bearing in mind as to how long we were prepared to be in exile. The only difference between us and Idi Amin-Dada was that he had military skills and armed to the teeth; why couldn't we acquire military skills, arm ourselves to the teeth and even scores with him? I would ask myself as to how long we were going to entertain Idi Amin-Dada's misrule. I and others of like mind opted to acquire military skills to embark on an armed struggle to free ourselves and the entire country from his misrule. This was the only language Idi Amin-Dada would understand.

I was not happy however at the way most of our elites who were in exile responded to the call for the armed struggle when we proposed the idea. Since 1971, our elites had seen the danger of the power of the gun falling into the hands of ignorant, treacherous and brutal leaders like Idi Amin-Dada and their bed-fellows.

I was shocked to see that these elites in exile because of Idi Amin-Dada's regime, though not well versed in military matter, shrinking away from scene of duty, cowering in corner and leaving the conduct of military affairs against Idi Amin-Dada to men intellectually and morally their inferior.

They all knew that since 1971 Uganda had suffered serious internal troubles. I expected men of good will among us to realise that in times of trouble like that, Uganda's reliance must be largely upon the soldiery of her citizens. Our elite therefore could have responded to this honourable call favourably. However, they told us without shame that they would only participate at another level when Idi Amin-Dada has been ousted from power. Yet I expected them to join the armed struggle willingly given the opportunity that had availed itself.

If Uganda elites had joined the armed struggle massively, I thought this would ensure that the power of the gun would not fall again into the hands of ignorant, treacherous, and brutal leaders in Uganda after the departure of Idi Amin-Dada.

Dr Henry Kissinger, the former Secretary of State of USA[26], once said that:

> "... if the fight for truth is taking place and all men of honour are on the ground armed on one is or the other, and you alone were to lie on your balcony an smoke your pipe out of noise and danger, then you had better have died or never have been alive at all than such a sensual coward..."

This quoted comment has been so true to many of our elites in exile because of Idi Amin-Dada's regime and, as it were, not concerned at all, about how they are going back to their country. While on the other hand their more patriotic fellow citizens will be in the battlefield battling it out for freedom for all Ugandans.

Our older generation and generations before them made sacrifices so that we could be a free society and belong to a community of nations which seeks to solve disputes by civilized means. Since 1971 to date (1977) the same responsibility has fallen on us the younger generation. We know the formidable tasks that face the fighting men. Our cause is just. This is the cause of freedom and liberty and rule of law. The price we shall pay will be the blood of patriotic men who shall fall on the battle field; those who have been brutally murdered in the military barracks and elsewhere already.

Most of our elites in exile prefer self-advancement and pursuit of material things. The great truth is that material gains or benefits are not the highest things in civilization but understanding the marvels of nature, and respect of human values and dignity.

In due course we got to know those who were championing this course of confronting the Idi Amin-Dada military regime. At the beginning, we got to know Engineer Akena p'Ojok[27] and Engineer Okello Nokrach. They whispered to us that the

---

[26] 1973-77 under the USA Presidency of Richard Nixon.
[27] See notes 4

destination was Tanzania. When everything was set, we began leaving Nairobi for Dar es Salam in groups of three or four. At this juncture we got to know Flight Engineer Jack Oita Alecho who was based in Nairobi and working with East African Airways[28] (EAA). We also got to know Mr Apollo Ejou[29] then based in Arusha.

From Arusha, Mr Apollo Ejou would come to Nairobi to link up with Flight Engineer Jack Oita Alecho who would take the trainees in his blue Alfa Romeo to Namanga border post between Kenya and Tanzania and drop them there. Mr Apollo Ejou would take the trainees in his charge across the border to Tanzania and hand them over to the Tanzania military Intelligence[30].

The day we left Nairobi for Dar es Salaam, as I have already stated, Engineer Jack Oita Alecho drove us from Nairobi to the Tanzania/Kenya border of Namanga. In companion was Mr Apollo Ejou who came from Arusha to take us to Tanzania. From the border the Tanzania military intelligence officer put as in a Taxi which took us to Arusha. From Arusha we boarded a night express bus, which took us to Dar es Salam. On arrival, we were taken to guest houses under the President's Office. The arrangement was so smooth such that everything happened without any flaw.

We stayed in Dar es Salam for about two weeks waiting for others who were still to come from Nairobi and from Uganda. At the guest house, we exchanged pleasantries with one another and began to mentor each other about the important step we had taken. Those of us who were already in exile warmly welcomed those trainees who came from inside Uganda.

One day towards the end of March 1977 when all the 49 of us were assembled in Dar es Salaam, we headed for our training

---

[28] EAA wound up in 1977
[29] a former intelligence officer with General Service Unit (GSU) during Obote's first regime.
[30] See SUM Operational Epi-centre 1977-1979 – appended in back pages.

camp. Our training camp as we learnt later was based in Morogoro Region[31]. That day was that we were driven in two mini buses along a highway for about two hours. The mini buses slowed down when they came across a parked military LandRover[32] beside the highway. A Tanzania Peoples Defence Force [TPDF] Captain was standing outside the parked LandRover. He entered the parked LandRover upon seeing the two mini-buses and beckoned us to follow him. We followed his LandRover into a feeder road which led us to a Prison complex. We by passed it, then gained a path and drove along it into the bush which led up to a training camp. We were destined to stay here for about a year.

Our training camp was in a hidden place in a thick forest. It was situated in a semi-a loop of a meandering river. One would enter the camp like entering a beehive situated in a hole on an anti-hill. The camp was composed of three tents. The drivers of the mini buses just dropped us there and headed back to Dar es Salaam. We were left under the charge of a team of instructors who were destined to train us.

The team of instructors was headed by Capt. Kaluzi, with Sergeant Habby as his second in command, followed by Corporal Muchagga and Lance Corporal Mwaipopo who was the driver of their LandRover. There was another Corporal whose name I cannot recall now.

Capt. Kaluzi welcomed us into the training camp expressing sincere hope that we knew what had taken us there. The team then carried out a roll call in order to know every one of us. They then began to distribute to every one of us military uniforms, ponzos, sleeping bags, blankets, sweaters, a pair of military boots, mess tins, and Self-Loading Rifles [SLR][33] as a personal weapon for every one of us.

---

[31] See appended map in back pages
[32] a car brand of British manufacturer that specialises in four-wheel-drive vehicles for rough terrains.

After this, we discarded our civilian clothes for military uniforms. We then went for supper which the team had prepared for us. The instructors then left us in the evening and went to their barrack which was seemingly far away from our training camp. They told us that they would come back early the following morning to begin training us.

---

[33] type of firearm which fires a single shot with the pull of a trigger and uses the energy of that shot to reload the chamber for the next round.

4.

OUR TRAINING

Our instructors came very early the following morning as they promised. This became a routine during our training; and each morning they came along with our rations of the day. It was only on Saturdays when they doubled our rations to cater for Sunday as well. They maintained the diet we were getting at the Guest House in Dar es Salaam. Capt. Kaluzi saw to it that we had additional supplies of meat from game meat. He was a good shot such that I cannot remember how many antelopes or warthogs we ate while we were in the training camp.

On arrival, each morning, they took us for a run of about 10 - 15 km. We came back from the morning run, brushed our teeth, washed ourselves, dressed up, and then went for breakfast. As breakfast, we took tea with milk or porridge with two buttered slices of bread. After breakfast, we fall in for our parade, at a clearing in front of the camp. At the beginning of the parade, they inspected our smartness in uniforms, and the cleanliness of the barrels of our personal weapons. After all this, Corporal Yohamma would give us a brisk warm up that always took away whatever breakfast we had taken. Amid the rising dust we then fall off to proceed with the morning lessons of the day, meanwhile, three of our colleagues took care of our kitchen affairs for the day.

We began our rigorous military training under the keen leadership of Capt. Kaluzi. He taught literally everything in our basic military training. He had a wealth of military experience and had trained many liberators be it Zimbabweans, Angolans,

Mozambiquans and South Africans and we Ugandans now joined the illustrious list of those he trained. We started with weapon training. We were introduced to various small arms we would be destined to use in turn. We were first trained on how to use the Self-Loading Rifle (SLR). We were introduced to the SLR and got to know its various parts and how it works. We were shown how to dismantle and assemble it. Later we began competing in stripping and assembling it within a minute.

Once we had mastered the SLR we were introduced to the Automatic Kalashnikov [AK]-47 rifle, Light Machine Gun [LMG], Makarov Pistol[34], Grenades (both defensive and offensive) and finally we were introduced to Bazookas. We later shot all these weapons in the shooting practice at the range. Interwoven with our weapon training were war field crafts, obstacles crossing, recognisance, military tactics and strategy, types of camouflage, types of attacks, how to set ambushes, night attacks, surprise attacks, jungles range and so on.

Later we did land mine engineering, whereby we were introduced to various types of land mines and later letter bombs since they operate on the same principle. We learnt how the land mine works, how to set it, lay it and defuse it. We also learnt demolition thoroughly since we were told, it was going to be one of the means we were going to use to disable our enemies.

All in all, our basic military training was rich in content and bias towards military intelligence and land mine engineering. We went at it in all earnest since most of the trainees were young, physically fit, and had the minimum qualification of a General Certificate of Education [GCE] Level. We picked up what we were being taught fast enough and besides we were eager to acquire military skills so that we would sooner or later even scores with Idi Amin-Dada and his likes in Uganda.

---

[34] Russian made semi-automatic pistol.

As a routine our training involved morning and evening runs. After the morning runs, we brushed our teeth, bathed, dressed up and took breakfast, after which we went for morning lessons. After the morning lessons we broke off for lunch. After lunch, we fell in again for parade then proceeded with afternoon lessons after which we would go for evening runs, after which, we bathed and then went for our supper. Saturday was a half-day and Sunday was a rest-day unless there were lessons that required night time. Usually we were free at night; we devoted it for story-telling and sleeping.

Last but not least, our military training also involved political education. In political education we defined the enemies of Uganda then and mentored ourselves. In our political education lessons, we took time to look at post-independence political history of Uganda. During the political education lessons, we asked ourselves many questions and discussed many issues, which we tried to answer candidly to the best of our ability. Some of the questions are highlighted below:

QUESTIONS

The first question we asked ourselves was:

> "...What is the main problem of Uganda? In other words what was deterring us to live in peace and security and harmoniously?

[*See appended Notes 1 or a more elaborate summary of the dialogue*]

The second question we asked ourselves during our political lessons was:

> "...Why Idi Amin-Dada became President of Uganda without any competence to lead a country...?

[See appended Notes 2 or a more elaborate summary of the dialogue]

The third question we asked ourselves during our political education lessons and we tried to answer it candidly, was:

> "...Why Col Idi Amin-Dada could not be stopped by Dr Apollo Milton Obote from staging his coup, when it was open secret that Idi Amin-Dada was working at it?..."

[See appended Notes 3 & 4 or a more elaborate summary of the dialogue]

The fourth question we asked ourselves during our political education lessons was:

> "...How Col. Idi Amin-Dada maintained himself in power after ousting Dr Apollo Milton Obote from power...?

[See appended Notes 4 or a more elaborate summary of the dialogue]

5.

VISITS OF OUR TRAINING CAMP

One Saturday of September 1977, Mr Apollo Ejou and Mr Dennis Echwou[35] visited our training camp. Dennis Echwou, a lawyer, was one of our leaders based in Uganda coordinating activities of our organisation with its leaders based in Kenya and Tanzania.

He was responsible for recruiting almost all our trainees from inside Uganda[36]; so, it was those of us who were in exile who did not know him. Those trainees directly recruited from Uganda knew him well. All the same, Mr Apollo Ejou introduced Mr Dennis Echwou to us. Mr Apollo Ejou told us that that they have come to find out how we are faring with our training.

Mr Dennis Echwou told us that Uganda was ripe for change, therefore very badly and urgently needed our inputs to bring about change. However, on a sad note, he told us that he witnessed the public execution of the so-called conspirators which took place in September 1977.

He told us that four were gallant sons of Uganda who had put their lives on the line, for the love of their country. Their public execution, he said, should encourage us about the need to bring about change in Uganda then. Mr Dennis Echwou told us that the four were publicly executed against the plea of Islamic leaders in

---

[35] Post-Amin served as a member of the National Consultative Council (NCC) 1979-1980; then Member of Parliament (MP) 1980-1985; also Chairman of the Board of Directors for the Immigration Board and also of Uganda Airlines Corporation 1980-1985.
**Was assassinated late 1985 during the Okello/Okello Military regime.
[36] See Flagpost 2 – map of Uganda

Uganda that executions should not be carried out during Ramadan[37]. Mr Dennis Echwou appealed to us to train hard to acquire the requisite military skills that would enable us to bring about political change in Uganda through armed struggle, since there was no other means of doing this.

Mr Dennis Echwou told us that since Idi Amin-Dada came to power on 13th February 1971; all attempts to oust him from power by force of arms had failed because the political conditions prevailing in Uganda were not ripe for change besides the sectarian nature of such attempts. He went ahead to state that the only hope for change in Uganda then was in us, since we were using a broad-based approach to do so. He asked whether we were equal to the task.

The visits of the two boosted our morale so much. They stayed with us the whole of that Saturday afternoon. We assured them that we were ready to put our lives on the line for our country. God willing, we were going to contribute in ousting the tyrant out of power. They then left for Dar es Salaam late in the evening.

Another event which boosted our morale immensely was when Uganda reached the football Africa Cup of Nations final for the first time. The Uganda's Cranes[38] lined up against Ghana's Black Stars but lost 0-2. Mr Phillip Omondi of Uganda team, '...*The Cranes*...' was voted the best player of the tournament with nine goals to his credit. Our instructors brought a transistor radio in the training camp to enable us to follow the match live!

Another event, which boosted our morale was the formation of Uganda National Movement (UNM) in Lusaka, Zambia in August 1977 with Mr John Barigye[39], Uganda's former ambassador to

---

[37] the ninth month in the Islamic calendar, observed by Muslims as a month of fasting.
[38] The name arises from the Uganda's national emblem bird the Crested Crane, hence the national football team '...*The Cranes*...'
[39] was a Prince to the Ankole throne/Monarchy abolished in 1966. Post-1986, under the Museveni-NRA regime all monarchies were restored except the

Bonn as Chairman, but later replaced by Mr Edward Rugumayo[40]. We did not lack knowledge of any current affairs because our instructors used to update us of any prevailing affairs of any importance to us.

However, the collapse of the East African Community (EAC) was one of the events, which hit us so low. EAC finally ceased to exist in July 1977 and Uganda then set about establishing government corporations such as Uganda Railways Corporation (URC), Uganda Airlines Corporation (UAC), and Uganda Posts and Telecommunication Corporation (UPTC), among others.

Time was flying so much such that we did not notice its passing because we were too busy to notice it. I recall, however, one morning, in the course of our weapons training on the Bazooka[41] Rocket Propelled Grenade [RPG][42], a weapon introduced to us with sufficient explanation given as how it works. Next, was the demonstration in shooting it, and Mr Richard Nonno was given the honourable task of doing so. The target was a giant baobab tree. He loaded the RPG and shot it hitting the branch of the tree. What a deafening sound it gave. Unfortunately, one of its shrapnel landed on my thigh creating a hole in my trousers as big as a coin and, as a consequence, left a white wound on my thigh. There was no blood for some time but just white fatty tissue. Iodine medicine was thereafter immediately applied on it. I felt a lot of pain on the spot for a long time even then when the wound had healed. That was the first experience I had with the RPG.

We continued with our training in earnest and 1977 passed almost unnoticed by most of us. However, one day of January

---

'Omugabe' of Ankole for unknown and unclear reasons.
[40] Emerged as Chairman of the National Consultative Council (NCC), a component of the post-Amin ruling Uganda National Liberation Front (UNLF).
[41] portable recoilless anti-tank rocket launcher weapon.
[42] shoulder-fired anti-tank weapon system that fires rockets equipped with an explosive warhead.

1978, we got another visit, this time by the Tanzania Peoples Defence Force (TPDF) Director of Training. He came in tow with a Capt. Simbeyi from State House, who was directly responsible for our training, and one of our commanders, Col. Zedekiah Maruru[43].

The director looked at our faces and told our instructor that our faces were then faces of soldiers. He thanked us for the enduring spirit we have demonstrated during our training. He thanked our instructors for struggling with us up to this level. He wished us the best of luck in our endeavours. Col. Zedekiah Maruru too thanked us for our perseverance and for volunteering for this historic mission. It was also a Saturday. Their visits were brief but nevertheless left us in high spirits with the assurance that we were almost through with our training.

There is one thing – I need to mention about visits in our training camp; they always came as a surprise. By January 1978, we had apparently completed our training because from then onwards we kept on revising what we had already learnt. One morning we were doing a drill in bayonet fighting, as usual the tasks master Corporal Yohamma. We stretched bayonet by the end of barrels of our personal weapons and took defence position for bayonet fight in:

'...Defend Yourself with bayonet...',

Corporal Yohama ordered.

'...Pierce one enemy in front of you with a bayonet...',

---

[43] Airforce Commander under Idi Amin Regime 1975-1977; under Uganda National Liberation Front (UNLF) - 1979-1980 was a Brigadier and as a member of the ruling Military Commission.; post-1985 to 1986 - as Major General was Uganda Army Chief of Staff.

**1976-1977, was central in the design and personal tutorial to Mwalimu Julius Nyerere of the SUM operational plan drown out and approved in 1977. This was rolled out successfully by the Tanzania Peoples Defence Force (TPDF) 1978-79; and delivered on schedule on April 9, 1979, at 730am, East African Time (EAT).

he shouted with voice echoing in the sky.

'...Cha up...'

we shouted in demonstration.

'...Attack two enemies one behind the other in front of you...',

he shouted.

'...Cha up, up, up, cha up...',

we shouted in demonstration.

'...Attack three enemies in front of you, one behind the other...',

he ordered.

'...Cha up, up, up, cha up, up, up, cha up...',

we shouted back in demonstration

The drill in bayonet fight went on and on such that we were exhausted. I began wondering when we shall go back to Uganda, now that we were ready for Idi Amin-Dada. I did not obey some of the orders and stood still. The corporal was furious with me. He told me that if I was a Tanzanian trainee, I would be one of the 10%. By this, he meant I would be beaten to death because 10% of their trainees could die during training and this could not be questioned by military authority.

I do not know what madness came in my head that day. I asked Corporal Yohama when we were going back to Uganda to face Idi Amin-Dada instead of shouting '...cha up! Cha up!...' Amin and his cronies are having a field day finishing our people, I continued. Corporal Yohama was furious with me! He began lecturing all of us. He told us that Tanzanians were not happy about the state of affairs in Uganda. But whatever indiscipline we were demonstrating was not helpful in any way. As it were Tanzania will continue enjoying their freedom as usual. The onus was on us to work hard to get rid of Idi Amin-Dada. This was what they were helping us to do. My colleague ordered me to behave and I saw sense. Then Corporal Yohama called off the drill of bayonet fighting, and we went to lunch.

We continued with our training up to February 1978. One day, our instructors told us that our training was now over. There was no fanfare about it because there was no pass out parades. That evening we returned back our personal weapons, military uniforms, mess tins, sleeping bags, blankets and ponzos[44]. We put on our civilian clothes and trekked on for about 5 kilometres where we found two mini-buses which took as back to Dar es Salaam. In Dar es Salaam we were taken back to a guest house, which belonged to the State House, where we stayed for some time. Then later, we were taken to Munduli Town near the Tanzanian Military Academy of Munduli.

In Munduli Town we first went in a lodge whereby we were more or less on holiday. Later on, we were transferred to a guest house in Munduli Town, and there, our security was in the hands of a Major Mawiya and Capt. Daniel of TPDF. Once we were in Munduli we were free to interact with the ordinary Tanzanians. They were always curious about where we were coming from and what our motive was. Were we friends or foes? I took note of the fact than any average Tanzanian was a security conscious person. We interacted with civilians in Munduli whenever went for prayers on Sunday in the Lutheran Church. All the same we could not tell them that we were Ugandans.

One day of early march 1978, we got another surprise visits from our leader Col. Zedekiah Maruru who was flanked by another of our commanders Col. William Omaria L'orapai[45]. Then another by Mr Dennis Echwou and Mr Apollo Ejou and was now flanked by Mr Ateker Ejalu[46] and Engineer Akena P'Ojok[47]. They

---

[44] Swahili word for a military overcoat to protect one from rain and cold.
[45] Was Brigade Commander under Idi-Amin regime up to 1976; then a member of the ruling Military Commission, a component of the Uganda National Liberation Front (UNLF) 1979-1980, a Member of Parliament/Deputy Minister of Internal Affairs 1980-1985.
[46] Was Editor-in-Chief of the People Newspaper up to 1971, then Information

thanked us immensely for the patriotic spirit we demonstrated. They warned us to desist from a sectarian spirit. They told us that we were homeward bound. They apologised about the early infiltration into Uganda by our combatants which proved to be a misadventure. Added that the earlier infiltration had been done without the knowledge and blessing of our political leaders in Nairobi, Kenya, and that matters had now been rectified. The said that misadventure led to the arrest of three of our combatants by Idi Amin-Dada's State Research Bureau (SRB) personnel. We later on learnt that they were badly tortured and taken to Idi Amin-Dada. Due to too much torture they told Idi Amin-Dada who they were and what their mission was!

During this early infiltration in April 1978, one of our combatants Mr Ray Okwir witnessed the accident in which Idi Amin-Dada's Vice President, Mustafa Adrisi was involved in a suspicious car accident. Idi Amin-Dada had earlier accused his Vice President Mustafa Adrisi of retiring a Commissioner of Prisons and 3 senior prisons' officers. In the vicinity of this suspicious car accident involving Mr Mustafa Adrisi, our SUM fighter, Mr Ray Okwir was in a taxi behind the Vice President's convoy. Mr Ray Okwir was armed but could not do anything because during training we were warned that The President and his Vice President were big and complex targets that we were not trained to hit lest we abort our mission.

Later, whatever mistakes that was there was rectified. After that visit, we began infiltrating Uganda once more. We left in groups of three and four. Further infiltration into Uganda took place with the knowledge of our political leaders based in Kenya.

Secretary at the East African Community (EAC) Secretariat in Arusha, Tanzania up to 1979; a member of the ruling Central Executive Committee (CEC)/Minister of Industry, a component of the Uganda National Liberation Front (UNLF) 1979-1980; Managing Director for Uganda Railways Corporation until 1985; Minister of Labour under the National Resistance Army (NRA)-Regime 1990

[47] See Flagpost 5

The Tanzanian military intelligence saw to it that we were provided with Identity Cards (IDs) and graduated Tax Receipts for Kampala City Council (KCC) for 1976, 1977 and 1978. They bought for us executive shirts and trousers such that we looked very presentable. If Idi Amin-Dada's SRB personnel were looking for bearded and shabbily dressed guerrillas, they were mistaken

When it was my turn to infiltrate into Uganda, there were four of us. Upon reaching Nairobi with Apollo Ejou, we met Engineer Akena P'Ojok[48] who was in the company of Prof. Ephraim Kamuntu[49], then a lecturer at the Nairobi University. We met them in the morning, I therefore had ample time to look for Mr Justine Ocitti and Mr Seraphina Olaa, two of my colleagues with whom I came to exile in Kenya. I found that all of them had enrolled for Master's Degrees at Nairobi University in their various fields of specialities. I met only Mr Justine Ocitti who was at the same time teaching mathematics at Nairobi School. I told Mr Ocitti that I was homeward bound. He looked at me and said nothing. I was staying at Trinity College Eastleigh with both Mr Justin Ocitti and Mr Seraphina Olaa as I have stated before. They knew of my departure for somewhere. He only wished me good luck!

At night, one of our leaders drove us up to Busia, a border town between Kenya and Uganda. There we looked for Mr Opio upon crossing to Uganda side. Mr Opio was one of our agents based in Busia town. He was an Immigration Officer of Uganda. We found Mr Opio with Mr Moses Musoke, one of our combatants who had already infiltrated Uganda. Mr Moses Musoke told us

---

[48] See Flagpost 5
[49] SUM codename was 'Prof'; SUM scribe/archivist 1973-1979, and served as member of the ruling National Consultative Council (NCC), a component of the Uganda National Liberation Front (UNLF) 1979-1980 and Minister of Supplies; thereafter 1980-1985 Member of Parliament (MP)/Ambassador Extra-ordinary plenipotentiary, Office of the President; thereafter Managing Director of Nile Bank and; post-1990 variously Minister of Environment/Tourism under the National Resistance Army (NRA)-Regime and Member of Parliament (MP).

that out route were clear. We crossed into Uganda through '...*panya*...'[50] route and travelled in a taxi with him up to Jinja, since our hosts were in Jinja. At Jinja, my host was Mr Oyoo who was working with the National Water and Sewerage Corporation. He was staying in Mufumbira near Namulesa on Kamuli Road. For that night, Mr Oyoo accommodated two of us, me and Mr Dimie Mayoni. We felt at home with him.

---

[50] Swahili word of a non-descript and secret route/entry paths; See Flagpost 3 - SUM Operational Theatres.

6.

FERRYING AND RECEIVING THE 'BLACK MARKET' GOODS

While we were going through our training in Tanzania, our leaders based in Nairobi had already taken care of transportation of arms, ammunition and explosives for our use up to Sega Lodge on the Kenya side of the border[51]. After I had infiltrated Uganda and was still based in Jinja, Mr Dennis Echwou[52] took me to where these items were being kept, in Jinja.

The challenge we had then was in transporting the consignments to Uganda to their various destinations. Engineer Quinto Ouma was handy in this respect. He was working with Uganda Electricity Board (UEB) and based in Mbale Town. Uganda exports electricity to Kenya from Owen Falls Dam, Jinja Town. Engineer Quinto Ouma's responsibility was to ensure a smooth flow of electricity to Kenya non-stop. He happened to be one of our political leaders based in Uganda. He was tasked with transporting the consignments of arms, ammunition and explosives into Uganda.

Hence, in the course of his duty, Engineer Quinto Ouma kept ferrying the consignment to Uganda. One evening, I saw Mr Dennis Echwou arriving with Mr Quinto Ouma in a brand-new Honda Civic car at Mufumbira where I was staying. The car which was driven by Quinto was full of our '...*Magendo*...'[53]: our small arms, ammunition, stabs of TNT[54], explosives, detonators and

---

[51] See SUM Operational Theatres 3
[52] Ibid 35.
[53] Swahili language/word description for black market goods; Ibid 40.

detonating fuses. Our consignment was mixed with real black-market goods like soap, sugar and salt. With the consignments they brought cartons of Key soap, giant packets of Omo soap; a bag of sugar and a bag of salt. Makarov Pistols[55] were sealed in giant packets of Omo soap, and some in cartons of bar soap; and bathing soap had ammunition, TNT slabs, detonating cords, fuses, detonators and grenades.

I was elated when they informed me on their arrival that they had brought my consignment of '...*black market goods...*' We went about ferrying the goods into the bungalow where we were staying. With the receipt of the goods, my major pre-occupation was in tendering to the compound. I slashed grass and took care of flower beds so well in the compound. I buried our explosives in holes I made in the flower beds and kept items that could be affected with water in secure places in the house.

With the arrival of our consignment I visited those who were hosting our combatants in Jinja such that I got to know all of them. One of them was **Mzee Otoa**[56], who was working as a telephone operator with **British American Tobacco (BAT)** in Jinja. Later on, Mzee Otoa took care of our communication with our leaders based in Kenya. Our leaders would ring him to inform us what to do. We would also inform Mzee Otoa to tell our leaders about our needs. I do not know how we could have communicated with Nairobi without him incurring any costs.

While I was in Jinja, my older brother Mr John Okoya [RIP] based in Kampala did not know that I was in Uganda. Mr Thomas Oringa, one of our combatants and my nephew went to Kampala without my knowledge. He was eager to go and meet his woman friend Ms Jeroline Apio. Ms Jeroline Apio and Mr John Okoya were then tenants of Nakawa estate. The appearance of Mr

---

[54] Trinitrotoluene - a pale yellow, solid organic nitrogen compound used chiefly as an explosive
[55] Ibid 34.
[56] see appended Notes 5

Thomas Oringa at the estate created a lot of concern at the beginning. Those who knew Mr Thomas Oringa and knew he was in exile wondered what he had come back to Uganda to do. Mr Thomas Oringa had to explain to them what he was up to. He even informed my brother that I was already in Uganda but based in Jinja.

My brother Mr John Okoya travelled thereafter to Jinja with the intention of meeting me but he was unable to do so. He however went back to Kampala with the assurance that I was really in Jinja, to satisfy his curiosity. Later on, I received an order from Nairobi that I should take command of my colleagues based in Jinja and Kampala. At the same time Mr **Kenneth Kaunda Banya**[57] was ordered to travel to Kitgum to take command of veterans who were mobilised through the effort of Mzee Luka Lanek[58] [RIP].

Arms and munitions from Sega Lodge were transported to Kitgum through the effort of Mzee Luka Lanek.

At the beginning, of our infiltration, we thought that our base of operation would be in Jinja. Later on, we saw the need for transferring our base of operation to Kampala at Q10[59] of Nakawa estate. At this juncture, one may wonder as to how we managed to infiltrate into Uganda and succeed in carrying out all activities without any let up.

I would like to state that we succeeded in doing what we did in the first place because of the level of our training. The Tanzanians trained us as a special force that was capable in undertaking what we did. As a result, we outwitted Idi Amin-Dada's State Research Bureau (SRB) personnel most of the time. Another opportunity we had was timing. The economy of Uganda

---

[57] See Flagpost 1
[58] See Appended Notes 6.
[59] Q is a short code for Quarter. This applied to government residential estates for Mid-lower-level workers, hence the coding of each house in the estates as 'Q'.

then was already in shambles and by 1978 Ugandans had already had enough of Idi Amin-Dada and they were really yearning for change.

We must remind ourselves that on 25th January 1978, Idi Amin-Dada declared 1978 as a year of;

'...*peace and reconciliation for Ugandans...*'

On the same date, there was the first meeting of the National Forum since its announcement in August 1973. National Forum was ostensibly meant to prepare Uganda for democratic rule. In March 1978, Idi Amin-Dada set up a Human Rights Commission (HRC) to both advise him and explain Uganda's image abroad. However, this was followed by the murder of the Industrial Court President, Mr Sebugwawo Amoti, and Mr Matthew Obado[60] (former Idi Amin-Dada's Government Minister). And earlier on in May 1977, ten-house system for control and surveillance of '...*tax evaders and rumourmonger...*' was inaugurated. These measures had their effects of deferring Ugandans from looking at one another as enemies. They served to reconcile Ugandans to a certain extent. They therefore played in our favour. By 1977, Idi Amin-Dada had learnt that some Ugandans were of no threat to his regime. Yet because of some trivial matters between such persons and his security agents, they were being innocently persecuted. He warned such errant operatives and Ugandans generally not to use his government in solving their trivial social issues.

Hence, as a result, by 1978, these measures had their desired effects. As a result, Ugandans had stopped settling scores among themselves using Idi Amin-Dada's security operatives. Specifically, they stopped reporting on matters they could not substantiate. So, 1978, was indeed a year of '...*peace and reconciliation for Uganda...*' as far as our infiltration was

---

[60] Ibid 21.

concerned. We went about our business unhindered by baseless reporting to security agents by Ugandans[61].

Another factor which played in our favour was the age and smartness of our combatants. Our combatants were generally composed of youth of school going age and were carrying school identity cards. They were generally smart, were clad in their uniforms, and could not attract suspicion. As for me, I was always clad in my French suit carrying a beautiful Samsonite briefcase, designed for businessmen with a super tough ABS shells with a glass fibre reinforced polyamide frame. I was more of a business executive than a guerrilla commander. I did not have any problem of identification because my identity card as a teacher of Kololo Senior Secondary School was still valid.

Besides identity, Nakawa estate in Kampala was my home turf. Since I came to Kampala in 1966 to continue with my studies, I was staying with my brother Mr John Okoya at Q10 up to 1977. Tenants of Nakawa estate who knew me took me as a home boy. Nakawa Estate was my second home in Uganda.

Once Mr Dennis Echwou[62] and Engineer Quinto Ouma had delivered our black market goods at Mufumbira, near Namulesa, Kamuli Road, in Jinja[63], I set about transferring them to Q10 at Nakawa estate at my earliest convenience. With the help of the Assistant Commissioner of Uganda Police, Mr Okun [RIP], we managed to transfer all that was needed by our combatants in Kampala. I distributed them accordingly to all the combatants in Jinja and Kampala. It was all they needed for defending themselves and launching an offensive against Idi Amin-Dada's regime. I gave every one of them his Makarov Pistol as a personal weapon and enough munitions for their immediate needs. But the explosives and all its' components that I gave

---

[61] See appended Notes 7
[62] Ibid 35.
[63] See SUM Operational Theatre Flagposts 3 & 2

teams were supposed to carry out specific missions towards D-day.

We knew how to carry our personal weapons so well such that knowing we have any weapon was not easy by both Kenya and Uganda Police. I vividly recall that when we were ordered to withdraw back from Jinja and Kampala to Nairobi, Kenya Police detained us at Yala Police Station overnight. Two of us had their Makarov Pistol but these were not detected. The following morning when we were released to proceed to Nairobi, we departed with our weapons undetected. On another occasion, Mr Moses Musoke was arrested in a security swoop by Uganda Police in the suburb of Kampala and was taken to Kampala Central Police Station, but the police did not detect the Makarov Pistol on him. He called his brother who took the weapon home in the travelling bag Mr Moses Musoke was carrying on him during the arrest.

7.

IN THE OPEN MOUTH OF THE CROCODILE

Operating in Uganda as an urban guerrilla during Idi Amin-Dada's regime was not an easy matter. No wonder then, we were like flies in the open mouth of a crocodile. Crocodiles eat flies. They trap them by opening their mouths wide for some time allowing flies to settle in their open mouths. Once they feel that many flies have settled in their mouths enough to be eaten, they then close their mouths, trapping and eating them. But some flies that are quick enough would escape before the crocodile closed its mouth completely.

When we were operating in Uganda as urban guerrillas we were like quick flies in the open mouth of a crocodile. We were always on guard avoiding being caught by those brutal State Research Bureau[64] (SRB) personnel of Idi Amin-Dada. Our training as a special military force enabled us to be like chameleons to suit any given situation. Once in Uganda, we were well behaved by keeping peace through discipline, without attracting any suspicion whatsoever. Most of us were teetotallers and highly disciplined when going about our business. But there were challenges as some of us were not disciplined enough as they would drink alcohol in excess to the extent of causing us a lot of concern. Mr Thomas Oringa my nephew was one of them. He was another one! He was staying with his woman friend, Ms Jeroline Apio near me at Nakawa estate. Once drunk he could even beat up Ms Jeroline Apio. There was a time we even

---

[64] Ibid 4

contemplated doing away with him altogether. However, when the D-day was approaching he began to behave as expected. This is what saved his life otherwise we would have done away with him.

When D-day arrived most of the combatants had gone upcountry to their homes. There was no way I could contact them because I did not know their respective homes. Those combatants who were recruited directly from Uganda had gone back to their villages in the Teso sub-region[65], and even some who were recruited when they were already in exile had gone to their respective homes in either Gulu or Kitgum[66].

This made it difficult for me to assemble two to three combatants for each of the targets we had identified to hit. Hence, to hit certain targets I deployed only one combatant. I was not happy with this state of affair, but I had no alternative. I had to work with the few combatants who were available. I wondered what might have made them go upcountry to their homes when they had an urgent duty to do in Kampala – was it cowardice? But we had already banished fear or cowardice when we were infiltrating in Uganda. Fear could not take one anywhere since one could not go back to his mothers' womb where he would be a bit safe. Our duty was to face the tyrant with all the courage we would need[67].

---

[65] See Flagpost 2
[66] Ibid 65.
[67] See appended Notes 8.

8.

THE D-Day AND ITS EFFECT

On D-day we took Nyerere's invitation to Idi Amin-Dada challenging him to a boxing fight as Idi Amin-Dada wanted. We had chosen three targets to hit in Kampala which would disable Idi Amin-Dada's war efforts against Tanzania. By then I was at Nakawa estate staying with my elder brother Mr John Okoya at Quarter10. Later I was forced, in Kampala to move to F29 to create rooms for other combatants to stay with Mr John Okoya at Quarter10. I moved to F29 to live with my woman friend Ms Rachel Ayaa[68].

To go back a bit, towards the D-day, I met Flight Engineer Jack Oita Alecho with Airforce Pilot, Capt. David Omitta[69] in Kampala. We held a brief meeting in the Parking Yard in front of Uganda Railways Head Office. Flight Engineer Jack Oita Alecho gave me the order from our leaders in Tanzania and Kenya that we attack targets we deemed important to start the liberation war against Idi Amin-Dada. He informed me further that it was up to us to determine the D-day, but it was in a matter of two or three days. He gave me too about half-a ream of our propaganda leaflets which we had to leave near where we were to carryout sabotage elsewhere on the streets for publicity.

That day I parted company with Flight Engineer Jack Oita Alecho and Airforce Captain David Omitta in high spirits. At the back of my mind, I knew the sabotage is as good as done because we had already identified the targets for it.

---

[68] See Operational Theatres Flagpost 3
[69] Ibid 68

D-day:
- I, Mr Thomas Oringa, Mr Okello Lalur, Mr Ocaya Vincent Gongo and Mr Oketch Ojukwu were scheduled to hit target A: Cutting down a Uganda Electricity Board (UEB) pylon opposite Spear Motors near junction leading to Ntinda.
- Mr Collins Chope was to hit target B: Cutting down the Uganda Electricity Board (UEB) pylon on Bukoto Hill supplying electricity to Western Uganda.
- Mr Julius Oketta was scheduled to blow up the only reserve fuel tank at Total Oil Depot near Kibuli Hill.

As we prepared to move to our Target A from Nakawa Estate, my elder brother Mr John Okoya, insisted that he must go with us. My brother was a veteran of Kings African Rifles (KAR)[70] who participated in the 1955 Mau[71] uprising campaign with KAR. No, I did not want him to involve himself in this fight, but we failed to dissuade him, and he insisted on going with us, as such that we could not leave him. Every one of us was armed with a Makarov Pistol with enough munitions. Reaching our target, we tied two slabs of Trinitrotoluene[72] [TNT] explosive together and tied them at the four feet of the pylon. We inserted the detonators already connected to the detonating cord then connected to the igniters to the detonating cord. We set off the igniters then moved very fast to the Jinja Road Highway and crossed it.

We moved up to Nakawa Vocational Institute (NVI) then the TNT explosive we set began to explode. Then after a while, there was darkness since the power line from Jinja to Kampala had already been cut-off. We began trotting towards Nakawa Estate and wondering aloud about what had happened to other

---

[70] A Colonial multi-battalion British colonial regiment raised from the various British possessions in East Africa from 1902 until independence in the 1960s.
[71] 1952-1960 - rebellion/uprising against the white European settlers in Kenya. This was politically driven/dominated by the people of Kikuyu ethnicity.
[72] Ibid 53.

pedestrians we were meeting on the way; and what they were doing.

Within five minutes or so all targets were hit as scheduled at 21:00 hrs local time. We heard the explosion on Bukoto Hill then the huge explosion of Total Fuel/Oil Depot located on the foot of Kibuli Hill. We could see the flame the burning oil was giving from Total Oil Depot. So, it was *fait accompli!* Praise be to God on High! Long live Free Uganda.

By the time we reached the junction leading to Naguru, we saw Idi Amin-Dada's limousine meeting a LandRover of the Uganda's Inspector General of Police (IGP) Haj Kassim Musa Obura. Idi Amin-Dada asked him aloud about what had happened. We could not hear clearly what reply Haj Kassim Musa Obura gave Idi Amin-Dada because of attendant noise by other vehicles plying along Jinja Highway. Soon Idi Amin-Dada turned around and drove towards Kampala with Haj Kassim Musa Obura's LandRover in tow. There was total darkness in Kampala, light could be seen only where generators set them on.

Idi Amin-Dada when meeting Haj Kassim Musa Obura at Naguru junction was hardly seven metres away from us. He was within the effective range of our Makarov Pistols. But as I have already mentioned, our instructors told us not to try shooting Idi Amin-Dada because he was a big and complex target which we were not trained to attack lest our mission aborts.

From the Naguru junction we moved fast to gain Q10 in Naguru Estate. We found in the Estate, everybody was outside their respective houses wondering aloud what had happened. The reserve fuel Total Oil Depot on the foot of Kibuli Hill was burning slowly giving huge flames. Some people in the Estate were alleging that it was military planes from Tanzania which bombed all these targets. All sorts of allegation were being made but we knew best. Mission Accomplished! Glory be to the almighty God! My brother Mr John Okoya was highly elated when we gained Q10. He was so happy that he also had contributed in

this honourable effort to oust Idi Amin-Dada from power. He served in the Kings African Rifles (KAR) with Idi Amin-Dada during the Mau Mau[73] uprising in Kenya. That served him right! my brother kept on repeating this. After some time, every one of us retired to his respective places of abode.

On the day we carried out our mission, some of our combatants set about distributing our propaganda leaflets in Kampala. In our leaflets we stated that Save Uganda Movement (SUM) was everywhere all over Uganda; and that all Ugandans were members of SUM. In the leaflet, we asked all Ugandans to join us in this noble and historical struggle that will set them free. Our combatants in Jinja, once we had carried out the mission, they also distributed our propaganda leaflets[74]. Our combatants in Jinja distributed Save Uganda Movement (SUM) propaganda leaflets after our mission. In Kampala, when Makerere University students got our leaflets they wished we could contact them so that they could work together with us.

The next day there was no piped water all over Kampala. In the morning, from Nakawa Estate, we went collecting water from the fish pond in Kampala City Council (KCC) park at Lugogo with pails and jerry cans. The next day, very early in the morning there was security search for those who carried out the sabotage. The security search apparently took place all over Kampala and was carried out by the entire Uganda Armed Forces; Soldiers, Policemen and Prisons Warders. They demanded for Identity Cards (IDs) and searched houses briefly. A prison warder searched F29, that is, the house where I was living with my woman friend Ms Rachael Ayaa. He came when I was still in my pyjamas. He carried out a visual search and satisfied himself he left and went elsewhere.

After the security search, I kissed Ms Rachel Ayaa and thanked her for the brave spirit she had demonstrated. Then she laughed

---

[73] Ibid 71
[74] see Appended Notes 10.

it off. All the same, I thanked her repeatedly for what she had done. Once the inspection of the estate was through, I dressed up and went about visiting our combatants wherever they were in Nakawa and Naguru Estates. I found out that all fared well in their respective places of abode. How grateful I was about this to the Almighty God!

That day, Mr Julius Oketta called on me at Q10[75] towards noon. I cannot recall now for what reason. We congratulated one another immensely for the respective mission we have accomplished. I went with Mr Julius Oketta up to Kampala. When we reached Uganda House we stopped. While we were standing on the pavement on the roadside opposite Uganda Commercial Bank building, we saw Uganda Special Branch Officers going for their duty. They were certainly looking for us and moving in twos. Some wore Kanzus[76] with coats on top, carrying 'rapier' bags. They looked like people coming from rural areas. Many of them headed for 'OTC Bus Park' and Buganda Bus Park. We looked at them with a lot of amusement and wished them the best of luck in their endeavours.

I parted company with Mr Julius Oketta, and then proceeded to Bukoto street to check on Mr Collins Chope. Collins was staying with his sister married to my nephew SSP Cornelius Ouma [Senior Superintendent of Police], who was a senior CID Officer [Criminal Investigation Department]. We were very happy to meet one another and inquired from one another how our respective missions went and the challenges we met if any. Mr Collins Chope's brother-in-law looked at us with a lot of amusement. He joked with us that we were completely wrong characters. We told him we had to be such for the love of our country.

---

[75] Ibid 51
[76] infers to a long-flowing traditional men's wear during befitting occasions; adopted Arab gab.

SSP Cornelius Ouma, my nephew, then briefed us about Uganda Police CID strategy and deployment for netting us. We thanked him profusely for this. Most of our combatants were staying with Senior Police Officers. That being the case, it was not easy to get us. From information I gathered from these Senior Police Officers we resolved that we should lie very low until otherwise. I informed all combatants in Jinja and Kampala accordingly. I told them that we should not make any offensive but must be on constant alert to defend ourselves in case of any attack against us.

Later on, in the course of the week, one Criminal Investigation Department (CID) Officer, of Langi nationality, got wind of what we did. He threatened to arrest us. He normally came to Nakawa Estate for Malwa (millet-based beer) drink. But his fellow Langi warned him not to do such thing since we, were sent by Dr Apollo Milton Obote[77] to carry out that mission. They told him that if arresting us would make the Acholis and Langi who were killed by Idi Amin-Dada since 1971 to come to life he could do so. Well, after that advice, the man kept quiet. Glory be to the Almighty God! Amen!

After three days our combatants based in Jinja sent three of their colleagues to Kampala[78]. They wanted to know why I excluded them from carrying out their mission. I told them that they were scheduled to carry out their mission in the near future if need be. They were furious with me! I had to calm them down by telling them that our mission was their mission too. They should be gratefully that we carried out our mission successfully on behalf of all of us. I told them that time could not allow me to alert them about carrying out their mission, with what I told them they went back to Jinja in good spirit.

---

[77] Ibid 18
[78] See SUM Operational Theatres 3

After our mission Idi Amin-Dada told the world that his security men had arrested all those who carried out the sabotage mission and had executed all of them. But our spokesman in Nairobi told the world than none of us was arrested, that we were all sound and safe there in Uganda rearing to do more. Our spokesman appealed to all Ugandans to join the struggle to gain their freedom.

While we were in the *"...open mouth of the crocodile..."*, I interacted a great deal with our political and military leaders of SUM based in Uganda. To begin with, we had officers and other ranks in Idi Amin-Dada's army who were with us fighting within the army.

I will mention here three of them. There was Flight Captains David Omitta and Sam Walugembe[79] who were ace jet fighter pilots in the Airforce. When Idi Amin-Dada's MIGs started bombing Tanzania on 10th September 1978 and Amin ordered the bombing of Kyaka Village and Bukoba Town which were turned into ghost places on 28th September, Captains David Omitta and Sam Walugembe did not bomb any targets which they were supposed to bomb. If anything, they discharged their bombs in Lake Victoria. This is a fact which Ugandans did not know and I'm just disclosing it now.

There was also a tank technician by the name of Oyer[80]. He was at the rank of **Regimental Sergeant Major [RSM]**. RSM Oyer who was from the Mechanised Division of the Uganda Army during the war pre-occupied himself with removing firing pins of cannons of tanks while he was servicing tanks heading to the military front during the war. This helped in disabling some of Idi Amin-Dada's tanks during the war[81].

In my interaction with military leaders of SUM based in Uganda Army, and Uganda Airforce, I met Capt. David Omitta once. I

---

[79] Ibid 68
[80] See SUM Operational Theatres 3
[81] see appended Notes 11.

met him when he was in the company of Flight Engineer Jack Oita Alecho a few days before D-Day. The Flight Engineer introduced him to me. Flight Capt. David Omitta looked at me with a broad smile as if in my mind, he was wondering whether I was equal to the tasks ahead. All the same, we exchanged pleasantries. After the meeting they would take me for coffee at YWCA restaurant, at Lumumba Avenue[82].

I must also mention here others of our political leaders who were based in Uganda[83].

---

[82] see Appended Notes 12 & SUM Operational Theatres Flagpost 4.
[83] see appended Notes 13

9.

TOWARDS THE FALL OF IDI AMIN-DADA's REGIME

In December 1978, there were continued skirmishes and press attacks mainly from Uganda. An *Ad Hoc* Committee for Promotion of Unity among Ugandan in the diasporas was created. January 1979 passed by with the Catholic Church Centenary celebrated in a war atmosphere. There was the first major meeting of Ugandan in exile in Nairobi under the chairmanship of Prof. Tarsis Bazana Kabwegyere[84] of **N**airobi **D**iscussion **G**roup [**S**ave **U**ganda **M**ovement in reality] took place.

> On 12th January 1979, former President of Uganda, Dr. Apollo Milton Obote, released a 15-page statement in which he declared '...*I have no personal office in Uganda to gain or regain...*'
>
> On 19th January 1979, Dr. Obote, gave a press conference and called for a Uganda-wide rebellion but unity of opposition groups remained elusive.
>
> However, on 21st January 1979, Tanzania troops crossed the Uganda Border en masse.

In February, war intensified as **T**anzania **P**eoples **D**efence **F**orces [**TPDF**] with help of **K**ikosi **M**aalum (**KM**), **F**ront for **N**ational **S**alvation (**FRONASA**), **S**ave **U**ganda **M**ovement [**SUM**] and other

---

[84] SUM codename was 'TBK'. Post-Idi Amin served the UNLF-government as a Member of the National Consultative Council (NCC) 1979-1980, then went back to teaching at Makerere University 1981-1988, then from 1990 variously a Member of Parliament; Minister Relief, Disaster and Preparedness & then Gender, Labour and Social Affairs & General Duties in Office of the Prime Minister in under the Museveni NRA-regime.

smaller political groups progressed. Organisation of African Unity [OAU] attempts at mediation led by the 9-man ad hoc committee, under Maj. Gen. Henry Edmund Olufemi Adefope of Nigeria failed.

On 24th February 1979, Masaka and Mbarara were taken and then destroyed in revenge for the destructions by Idi Amin-Dada's army in the Kagera salient.

Massive recruitment of anti-Amin army in Mbarara was initiated by Mr Yoweri Museveni.

On 2nd March 1979, attack on the Tororo Air&Seaborne Battalion Garrison by anti-Amin forces (pro-Obote forces). Attack was led by Capt. Lorne Owere; was ex-Airforce and ex-East African Airways pilot; was recalled by the ancestors in 1995. It was Capt. Lorne Owere and Capt. Mvule who setup a SUM-cell in the Ex-Amin Airforce base in Entebbe 1975.

On 10th March 1979, Mr Yoweri Museveni back in Dar es Salaam from Mbarara, called for the unity of fighting forces.

On 24th March 1979, the Moshi Unity Conference began meeting behind closed doors at Moshi Police Training School.

Leading Uganda Peoples Congress [UPC] personalities such as Mr Adoniya Tiberondwa, Mr Sam Odaka, Mr Shafique Arrain, Mr Gurdial Singh and Mr Peter Otai were barred from attending the meeting. Mr Godfrey Lukongwa-Binaisa[85] too was barred.

On 25th March 1979, Uganda National Liberation Front [UNLF] is formed.

National Consultation Council [NCC] chaired by Edward Rugumayo was created. A National Executive Committee (NEC),

---

[85] Previous role as Attorney General in UPC/Obote-1 government 1962-1971

headed by Prof Yusuf Kironde-Lule was created. The Uganda National Liberation Army (UNLA) was also proclaimed (with its men already in Uganda).

> On 28th March 1979, Col. Muammar el Qadhafi issues an ultimatum to Tanzania to withdraw its troops from Uganda or face Libyan forces within 24 hours.

But how could someone trained to fight in the desert do well in a tropical environment? That was the question! So, the Libyan forces were no match to Tanzania Peoples Defence Force (TPDF) and their Uganda allies who were trained to fight in tropical environment.

By this time, Idi Amin-Dada was already on the run.

> On 3rd April 1979, through a Butebo Radio channel, Idi Amin-Dada dismissed as nonsense reports that he had fled and informed the nation of his determination to defend his '...*motherland*...'; as a Conqueror of the British Empire.

Idi Amin-Dada warned his cowardly officers and men of the consequences.

With these developments, it was evident that Mwalimu Julius Nyerere was going to knock out Idi Amin-Dada in their boxing contest. We fighters of SUM based in Jinja and Kampala were rearing to go as soon as the liberators reached Kampala. We were eager to go ahead with them to liberate unliberated parts of Uganda. However, it was at that moment that I received a contradictory order from our leaders in Kenya that we should withdraw to Nairobi. Come what may, we had to obey the order on the ground that our leaders knew best. We withdrew back to Kenya much as our hands were itching to even scores with Idi Amin-Dada's forces at the front lines.

On our way to Nairobi, Kenya Police detained us at Maseno Police Station. However, the next day, they set us free and we continued with our journey to Nairobi.

On 6th April 1979, there was heavy shelling of Entebbe by TPDF.

On 7th April 1979, a Libyan transport plane was set on fire by Tanzania troops at Entebbe Airport and Entebbe falls.

On 10th-11th April 1979, an attack spearheaded by the 19th Battalion of the 208th Brigade under Lt. Col. Ben Msuya and Brig. Mwita-Marwa respectively and assisted by the Uganda National Liberation Army (UNLA)[86] under Lt. Col. David Oyite Ojok takes Kampala.

Col. David Oyite Ojok announces end of Idi Amin-Dada's regime on radio Uganda and calls upon:

> '...masses in Uganda to rise up and join hands in eliminating the few remaining murderers...'

Prof. Yusuf Kironde-Lule was sworn in as President and announces formation of the provisional government, naming a Cabinet selected in Dar es Salaam. He then suspended all dealings in foreign exchange. It should be noted here that Flight Engineer Oita Alecho was delegated the responsibility for organising security for the swearing in ceremony of President Yusuf Kironde-Lule.

On 12th April 1979, Idi Amin-Dada using the Butebo Station, denounces Col. David Oyite Ojok's statement and then informed the nation that he was in control.

Looting and plunder of Kampala takes place. Idi Amin-Dada flees to Libya then to the Middle East.

On 23rd June 1979, Maj. Gen. Silas Mpunga's Task Force, which had continued fighting in the Western

---

[86] At start of the war in 1978, it was Kikosi Maalum (KM) but changed to UNLA in 1979 in line with the formation of the Uganda National Liberation Front (UNLF) in Arusha Tanzania.

Front along with Ugandan fighting groups, reached the Sudan border.

At last, Uganda was free once more!

After the fall of Kampala, we stayed in Nairobi for a week and half, and then we flew back to Entebbe in Uganda Airlines Fokker Friendship plane. Our flight back to Uganda was arranged by Engineer Akena p'Ojok[87] who was now a Minister in the Uganda National Liberation Front (UNLF) government. He was the leader of SUM[88]. While I was in Nairobi, I talked with Hon Akena p'Ojok on the phone. He informed me about the arrest of my brother Mr John Okoya by the notorious State Research Bureau (SRB) personnel.

On arrival at Entebbe airport, Uganda, we gained Kampala and what a rosy welcome we received from our leaders in Kampala! They were very happy to see us and many of them Ministers in the UNLF government of Yusuf Kironde-Lule. I asked Hon Akena p'Ojok whether we were going to the front lines to continue with the struggle. He told us that it was risky for us to do so. Why? he knew best! Never-the-less we were puzzled but we took a view he advised that time will tell.

We were given accommodation in some of Kampala's luxurious hotels. I was given a room in the Grand Hotel. I then went to Nakawa Estate to thank our hosts and what a rosy welcome we got. We found the Estate full of looted goods from warehouses and shops in Kampala. They showered us liberally with gifts of the looted items: executive shirts, wine and spirits from Winnits (U) Ltd, sugar from Food and Beverages, canned meat from Wankoko Army Depot on Port Bell Road, namely, anything shareable.

On a sad note, my elder brother Mr John Okoya narrated to us their ordeals at Nakasero, the headquarter of Idi Amin-Dada's

---

[87] See Flagpost 5
[88] See Flagpost 5.

notorious State Research Bureau (SRB). It was a place of no return once you were taken there. Mr John Okoya was arrested from Nakawa Estate at Q10 when we had left for Nairobi. He was arrested together with my brother in law Mr Paul Acama Oketch and one of our combatants Mr Oketch Ojukwu who remained behind because he was not with us when we were ordered to withdraw to Nairobi[89]

The same week when we came back to Uganda from Nairobi to Kampala Hon Minister Akena p'Ojok[90] organised a party at his suite- 214/215, in the Nile Mansions Hotel. This rendezvous was more or less a parade of who was who in SUM either from the diaspora and those based within Uganda. We had Hon Minister Akena p'Ojok, Hon Minister Ateker Ejalu[91], Hon Minister Prof Tarsis Kabwegyere[92], Hon Minister Yonasani Bankobeza Kanyomozi[93], Hon Minister Antony Ocaya[94], and Hon Minister Ephraim Kamuntu[95] who were then cabinet ministers in the Uganda National Liberation Front's (UNLF) provisional government. We had also SUM Military Commanders, namely, Col William Omaria Lo'Arapai and Col Zedekiah Maruru, who were representing us, (SUM, that is) in the Military Commission (MC) organ of UNLF.

Other members present were Hon Leander Komakech[96], Mr Okello-Okello, Mr Abednego Ongom, Mr Albert Lukwiya[97], Mr

---

[89] see Appended Notes 14 & Flagpost 4.
[90] See Flagpost 5
[91] Minister of Industry 1979-1980, under the Uganda National Liberation Front (UNLF) government; then under NRA-Regime was Minister of State for special duties in charge of pacification of the war-ravaged areas post 1988.
[92] Ibid 91.
[93] Served Uganda National Liberation Front (UNLF) as member of the National Consultative Council (NCC) 1979-1980; then 1980-1985 as Member of Parliament (MP)/Minister of Marketing and Cooperatives.
[94] Served Uganda National Liberation Front (UNLF) government as Minister of Planning and Economic Development 1979-1980
[95] Ibid 49
[96] Served the Uganda National Liberation Front (UNLF) as Member of the National Consultative Council (NCC) 1979-1980.

Jacob Okello Agwa[98], Mr Charles Alai, Mr Odoi Chwalle[99], Mr Dennis Echwou[100], Mr Apollo Egwau, Mr William Ekwaru[101], Electronic Engineer Leo Obwonyo, Flight Engineer Jack Oita Alecho, Dr Ojok Mulozi[102], Engineer Quinto Ouma, Mzee Luka Lanek, Dr Chotta Vuru, Dr James Ntozi[103] and nearly all combatants of SUM infiltrated into Uganda who were based in Jinja and Kampala[104].

This convergence enabled us to know one another and leaders of SUM we had never known. That was when we realized that SUM was a large family and a well organised liberation movement. I could recall so well that whatever action we wished to undertake moved princely like clockwork.

In the rendezvous I asked one question which was not answered by any of our leaders. I asked them about what we were going to do about our combatants who had died at the front-line and three who died in the hands of State Research Bureau[105] (SRB) personnel. Were we going to find out where their homes were so that we may go there to pay our last respects for them?

During this rendezvous we met our combatants who came with TPDF at the military frontline and it was not all joy when we learnt about how some of our combatants died at the front.

---

[97] Served as General Manager Uganda Transport Corporation (UTC) 1980-1986. Was recalled by the ancestor.
[98] See Thanks; Was recalled by the ancestors in Feb 2012.
[99] Continued as a Magistrate up to 1981; thereafter joined anti-Obote insurgency and was killed in one encounter.
[100] Ibid 34.
[101] Murdered 1979 on his way from Mombasa, Kenya while escorting Uganda's imports that had been held-up at the port because of the 1978/79 War.
[102] Elected Member of Parliament (MP) 1980-1985 for the Democratic Party (DP).
[103] Post-1979 was Chief Executive of the Uganda Bureau of Statistics and thereafter went back to teaching at Makerere University and is now retired.
[104] see appended Notes 15.
[105] Ibid 3

To begin with, there were some Ugandan soldiers and airforce men who were in exile in Kenya. They went to Tanzania to support the TPDF in the war against Idi Amin-Dada but they were not willing to go to the military front. They wanted to come through Lake Victoria to launch an attack on Entebbe. The TPDF granted them their wish and they set off from Mwanza or Bukoba in the Tanzania Marine Boats with some Tanzania Marines. When they reached a point where River Kagera flows through the Lake Victoria, the water current was too strong for some of the heavily-laden marine boats to go through the current. As a consequence, some of the boats heavily laden with weapons and ammunition sank in the Lake Victoria with Uganda combatants and Tanzanian marines.

In this mishap we lost one our dear combatant Mr Benjamin Coptic Ojok[106]. When Kampala was falling in the hands of liberators Idi Amin-Dada's troops were shelling the position of liberators on Mengo Hill and one of their mortar shells hit an overhead electric wire which fell on one of our combatants Mr John Okumu Samora and he died instant[107].

A few days after the rendezvous, we SUM fighters who were based in Jinja and Kampala assembled in the suite of Hon Minister Akena p'Ojok[108]. He then invited Army Chief of Staff of the Uganda National Liberation Army (UNLA) Lt. Col. David Oyite Ojok in his suite. He introduced us to him and requested him to co-opt us in the intelligence unit he was operating in his suite. Hon Akena p'Ojok assured Lt Col David Oyite Ojok that we may be of use to him because our training as a Special Military Force was biased towards military intelligence.

The UNLA Chief of Staff, Lt Col David Oyite Ojok promised that he would co-opt us in the intelligence unit he was operating[109].

---

[106] See Dedication; Flagpost 1 - no 19
[107] see appended Notes 16
[108] See Flagpost 5

Shortly after our rendezvous, one of our political leader Mr William Ekwaru who was based in Tanzania was heading home from Kampala to Soroti[110]. He did not reach Soroti. He disappeared on the way to Soroti. Later on, they found his dead body somewhere in Mabira Forest, located between Jinja and Kampala. His dead body was later taken home to Soroti for burial. The death of Mr William Ekwaru hit us so low and we kept wondering why it should happen when he had already reached Uganda safe and sound[111].

In the Uganda National Liberation Front (UNLF) provisional government we were well represented, and we had six ministers. In the Military Commission, a component of UNLF, SUM was represented by Col Zedekiah Maruru and Col William Omaria Lo'Arapai. We therefore had high hopes that our two commanders would take care of our interests of integrating in UNLA at all levels.

But when the time came for integrating all fighting groups into the UNLA we saw stars!!, when we went to Mubende Military Barracks for the integration into UNLA. None of our commanders even came to address us about how we were going to be integrated into the rank and file of UNLA. As I have already stated before, most of SUM fighters had at least 'O-Level' Certificate. They therefore deserved to be absorbed in the officer corps of UNLA.

But at Mubende Military Barracks we were excluded from this opportunity of pursuing military career as officers. Whereas fighters from Kikosi Maalum (strongly associated with Obote) and FRONASA[112] (of Yoweri Museveni's) were being sent for officers courses within and outside Uganda, to our detriment.

---

[109] see appended Notes 12 & 17
[110] See Flagpost 2
[111] see appended Notes 18.
[112] See appended notes 4.

APPENDICES:

NOTES: 1-18

Notes 1.

We noted with regret that Uganda was born with a major birth defect which we have to treat so that we may live in peace and harmoniously. This birth defect is our inability to meet the basic aspiration of the Baganda in whatever constitution we come up with for Uganda. We can only understand this best when we look at the way Uganda was formed right from the beginning by the British colonisers. The making of a sovereign nation of Uganda as we know it today began in 1864 when the British made a treaty with the Buganda Government, which process was accomplished in 1920; when the final Map of Uganda was drawn. During this period of 56 years the British made a number of treaties with other southern Kingdoms and annexed the northern parts of the present Uganda to southern states because these parts has been allocated to the British by the Berlin Conference of 1884. This was when Africa was divided among the then colonial powers of the day which were scrambling for Africa.

In their journals, the explorers reported to the British Foreign Office that, the Kabaka of Buganda was a powerful ruler, that his subjects were a settled people, and that the Kabaka had an administration similar to our own. Hence, as a consequence all subsequent actions of the British Colonial Empire were directed at building up a country later known as Uganda around Buganda Kingdom.

It is important to note that the British brought together independent Kingdoms and independent territories to form this geographical area which came to known as Uganda Protectorate after signing another treaty with Buganda Government, namely '...*The 1900 Buganda Agreement*...'

The British colonial Governors with assistance of the Kabaka of Buganda improved administration in other southern Kingdoms and established administration in other territories outside Buganda where organised government was not in existence. They improved on local administration outside Buganda by taking their (Buganda, that is) local administration structures from sub-parish, parish, sub-county and up to county level.

At upper level, the British Governors appointed District and Provincial Commissioners to represent them in the Kingdoms, and to administer directly the other territories to complete the colonial administration structure.

> On 1st August 1962 all parties at the Lancaster House, London, and last independence conference on Uganda signed the Independence Agreement.

Thereafter these independent states and territories willingly agreed to stay together at the departure of the British through the 1962 Constitution to which

> On 8th October 1962, this arrangement through Treaties and Annexations by which the British had grouped together states and Territories in this geographical area under the name Uganda Protectorate for trading purposes came to an end.

> On 9th October 1962, the Agreement for granting independence to Uganda came into force and this document brought into existence a political entity known as UGANDA.

The 1962 Constitution was a semi-federal constitution though it fell short after the basic aspirations of Baganda, nevertheless it accommodated most of their basic aspirations. In this Constitution, the Kabaka of Buganda remained as the ruler of Buganda.

From 1962 up to 1964, Ugandans lived in peace, security and in harmony enjoying their political independence. However, in July 1964 Bunyoro-Buganda conflict over lost counties, namely, Buyaga and Bugangaizi, intensified. It was resolved by all parties to the 1962 Constitution that the conflict of the Lost Counties between Bunyoro and Buganda should be decided by a referendum; that the Ugandans in the Lost Counties should decide where they want to belong. The President of Uganda, Sir Edward Mutesa-II[113] who was also the Kabaka of Buganda was accused of mobilising thousands of ex-service men for resettlement in Ndaiga in order to influence the outcome of the impending referendum over the "...*Lost Counties*..." The Kabaka of Buganda, Sir Edward Mutesa-II shot dead eight Banyoro in a market place in Ndaiga because they wanted to leave Buganda Kingdom and go back to Bunyoro Kingdom.

On 4th November 1964, the referendum over '...*lost counties*...' was held and the vote favoured the return of the counties to Bunyoro Kingdom.

In January 1965, the Kabaka of Buganda, Sir Edward Mutesa-II as President of Uganda refused to sign the instrument for transferring the '...*lost counties*...' into law.

Bad blood began developing between the President of Uganda, Sir Edward Mutesa-II and the Executive Prime Minister of Uganda, Dr Apollo Milton Obote[114] over the referendum for the '...*lost counties*...' This signified almost the end of Uganda Peoples Congress (UPC)/Kabaka Yekka (KY)-alliance. Thereafter, the politics of factionalism came into play in Uganda.

On 8th October 1965, assassination insinuations reached a climax as Dr Obote accused his Minister and Secretary General of the UPC, Grace K Ibingira of using

---

[113] Exiled to the United Kingdom in 1965; and recalled by the ancestors 1969
[114] Exiled second time in 1985 and recalled by the ancestors in 2005.

the '...*dollar*...', Sir Edward Mutesa-II of using foreign connections and Gen. Shaban Opolot, a section of the army, to overthrow the government.

The trio on the other hand accused Dr Apollo Milton Obote of attempts to eliminate them using Brig. Okoya and Col. Idi Amin-Dada.

On 9th October 1965, a third Uganda Independence Anniversary celebration took place at Kololo Airstrip. The Army Commander Col. Shaban Opolot, President of Uganda, Sir Edward Mutesa-II, and Minister of Justice and UPC Secretary General, Mr Grace Ibingira were all absent from the ceremony. As it were, an assassination attempt on Dr Apollo Milton Obote, who was present at the ceremony, was also alleged as led by a Maj. Ogwang.

In November 1965, Army Commander, Col. Shaban Opolot was accused of making army transfers in preparation for a coup. The Prime Minister, Dr Obote cancelled the transfers.

In December 1965, the President of Uganda, Sir Edward Mutesa, reportedly ordered for heavy weaponry and trucks through Gailey and Roberts Company with the intention of launching a coup d'état.

In 1966, Uganda entered the Buganda crisis. Mr Daudi Ochieng[115] 'KY' Member of Parliament (MP) for Mityana, alleged involvement of Col. Idi Amin-Dada, Ministers Mr Felix Onama, Alhaj Akaki Akbar Adoko Nekyon and Prime Minister Dr Apollo Milton Obote in the gold, ivory and coffee illegal business in the Congo[116].

---

[115] Was Parliamentary Opposition Chief Whip 1965-66; and Secretary General of the Kabaka Yekka (KY) Movement.
[116] The name changed to Zaire in 1971 and then to Democratic Republic Congo

In February 1966, Mr Daudi Ochieng, moved a motion in Uganda Parliament to suspend Col. Idi Amin-Dada from the army command, and institute a Commission of Inquiry[117].

By 5th-6th February 1966, there were allegations of plots and counter plots made by both Obote/Amin, and Mutesa/Ibingira/Opolot factions.

When Dr Obote returned from the East African Authority meeting in Nairobi, a top-secret meeting of Dr Apollo Milton Obote, Inspector General of Police (IGP), Erinayo Oryema, Secretary for Defence, Mr Wilson Lutara, Permanent Secretary of Internal Affairs Mr Oluoch and Dr Naphlene Akena Adoko of General Service Unit (GSU) resolved to arrest '...*coup suspects...*' and '...*assassins...*'

As a result, five Ministers were arrested while attending a cabinet meeting. The five Ministers were: Mr Grace Ibingira[118], Mr Balaki Keba Kirya[119], Mr George Magezi[120], Mr Mathias Ngobi[121] and Dr Emmanuel B.S. Lumu[122]. These were the main supporters of the Daudi Ochieng motion. The President of Uganda Sir Edward Mutesa-II was accused of having contacted British High Commissioner for military aid and Uganda Chief Justice for legal advice on how to fight Obote.

On 24th February 1966, the Prime Minister, Dr Apollo Milton Obote called a press conference at 7.00 pm and announced the suspension of 1962 Constitution and the post of President and Vice President[123].

(DRC) in 1997
[117] See Appendices Notes 1
[118] Minister of Justice 1962-1966.
[119] Minister of State Office of the President 1962-1966; and again, under NRA-regime 1986-1990. Recalled by the ancestors 1995.
[120] Minister of State for Housing and Labour 1962-1966.
[121] Minister of Agriculture and Cooperatives 1962-66 UPC/Obote-1; and again, under the Uganda National Liberation Front (UNLF) 1980.
[122] Minister of Health 1962-1966.

On 27th February 1966, Minister of Internal Affairs, Mr Basil Bataringaya[124], appointed a Commission of Inquiry into gold, ivory and coffee illegal business allegation.

On 15th April 1966, a new Interim Constitution nicknamed '...*pigeon hole*...' was introduced and passed by 54 votes to 4 making Dr Apollo Milton Obote Executive President of Uganda. Six of the twenty-one Buganda representatives in Uganda Parliament refused to take oath under the Interim Constitution.

On 18th May 1966, Chief Lutaya called Buganda Lukiiko at 10.00am, to convene.

On 20th May 1966, Buganda Lukiiko met to draft a motion not to recognise the Interim Constitution.

Members passed a motion that Central Government should remove itself and its institutions from Buganda soil, by end of the month. The then Katikkiro (Prime Minister) of Buganda, Mr Jehoash Ssibakyalyawo Mayanja-Nkangi[125], however, opposed the motion.

On 23rd May 1966, Government of Uganda ordered the arrest of Chiefs Lutaaya and Matovu.

Riots followed news of their arrest and Dr Apollo Milton Obote ordered Col. Idi Amin-Dada to take appropriate action.

---

[123] Was Mr William Wilberforce Kajumbula Nadiope, then also the Kyabazinga of Busoga.

[124] A Member of Parliament and the Democratic Party (DP) leader of opposition up 1965; and crossed over to join the UPC. Was murdered in 1972 by the Idi Amin-Dada regime.

[125] Before this served as a Member of Parliament (MP) for Kabaka Yekka and Uganda government as Minister without Portfolio 1962 – 1963; Later then as Minister of Education 1986 – 1989; 1989 – 1992: Minister of Planning and economic development; Minister of Finance 1992 – 1998; Minister of Justice and Constitutional affairs 1998 – 2002; Was recalled by the ancestors in 2012.

On 24th May 1966, Uganda Army fought a battle of Lubiri Palace forcing Sir Edward Mutesa-II to take refuge at Rubaga Cathedral from where he went into exile in the United Kingdom.

On 31st May 1966, Dr Obote addressed the nation justifying the army action as restoration of rule of law using fire.

In June 1966, Army Commander, Col. Shaban Opolot was arrested and detained; a state of emergency was declared over Buganda.

On 17th September 1967, Kingdoms were abolished, and Uganda became a Republic.

In January 1968, the Bulange building, which was the host Parliament and ruling citadel of the Buganda Kingdom, was sold to the Uganda Government Ministry of Defence for £250,000.

In September 1968, a Republican Constitution was introduced, and Dr Apollo Milton Obote as President was installed. Buganda was divided into districts and administered by District Commissioners. Former Kabaka Yekka (KY) Ministers, including Dr Samson B. Kiseeka[126], Mr Paul Lubega, Mr A.D. Lubowa[127], Al hajj Ntege-Lubwama[128] and Mr Francis Walugembe[129] joined the **Uganda Peoples Congress (UPC)**.

---

[126] From Buganda Kingdom Minister of Health and Works 1964 to 1966. Later Post-1986 served as Uganda Prime Minister under the NRA-regime.

[127] From the Buganda Kingdom Minister of Justice to Uganda government Minister of Health 1968-1971.

[128] From Buganda Kingdom Minister of Education; later 1977-80 served as General Manager Uganda Airlines; 1980-1983 as government Minister; then went into exile after an assassination attempt on his life.

[129] From Buganda Kingdom Minister of Natural Resources and under Obote-I (1962-71) was Mayor Masaka 1968-71 and was murdered under Idi Amin regime.

On 19th October 1969, an attempt was made to assassinate the President of Uganda Dr Apollo Milton Obote at Lugogo Indoor Stadium, Kampala.

Thereafter, political parties were banned, and State of Emergency was declared throughout Uganda.

On 21st November 1969, Sir Edward Mutesa-II died in exile in London.

On 25th January 1970, Brig. Pierino Okoya was murdered with his wife at their home in Gulu by an armed gang.

In September 1970, rivalry in the army and airforce was reported to have intensified between pro-Amin and pro-Obote factions.

On 9th October 1970, Dr Apollo Milton Obote was installed as Chancellor of Makerere University.

In this event, Col. Idi Amin-Dada appeared at the function unexpectedly. This was a breach of protocol and demonstrated a show of power on the part of Col. Idi Amin-Dada. It called for action to be taken to address such insubordination, but such prompt action was lacking on the part of Dr Obote.

The Constitutional change which took place in Uganda did not please the Baganda at all. From their point of view, the suspension of the 1962 Constitution in 1966 and its abrogation in 1967 by Dr Apollo Milton Obote and his associates; and using the army, and the police technically brought to an end the Uganda as a political entity which had been created willingly by member states and territories. According to them, from September 1967 the states and territories that formed Uganda were free, each to go its own way since there was nothing binding them together except the gun.

Buganda from 1966 to 1971 was ruled under emergency regulations by Dr Obote and thereafter by Idi Amin-Dada with the same policy from 1971 up to when Idi Amin-Dada left power in 1979.

The above arguments have been the position of the Baganda since 1967 when Dr Apollo Milton Obote abrogated the 1962 Constitution. And this has been the bone of contention in our Republican Constitution of 1967. The Baganda believe that since 1967, they have been denied human rights and had lived under excessive oppression. They want Ugandans to accept reality and recognise the fact that to permanently stop blood-spilling and destruction of property, we must go back and agree willingly to make a new arrangement based on the 1962 Constitution by which we shall live in peace, security and harmony forever.

They also want Ugandans to accept another reality that there are different nationalities/peoples in Uganda, as a consequence, the strength of our unity will be in '...*Unity in Diversity*...' They therefore call for a new constitutional arrangement which reflects the: Linguistic, Cultural, Ethnic and Social Diversity of the people of Uganda as absolutely necessary. This calls for a fully-fledged Federal Constitution.

The Baganda believe that, the people of Uganda have been hoodwinked by the '...*Unitarist Nationalists*...', yet Ugandans since 1967 have been living in the climate of suspicion, fear and greed. They point out that there must be adequate plans for addressing and managing Uganda's ills. They assert that our one need is the rise of a new spirit, a spirit above party politics, point of view, religion and personal advantage or gain. With this new spirit, they go on to assert that Ugandans can and indeed build a pattern of human cooperation among proposed Federal States and a national unity.

They argue that we must have justice whereby each one sees not only his/her difficulties but also the difficulties of the others. And that we must find that answer, which will give satisfaction and security to all – an answer that is above political party, that is above faction, which is above religion, which recognises our varied cultural heritage.

We saw that Baganda were therefore anxiously waiting from any would be statesmen and leaders of Uganda after Idi Amin-Dada, for those pronouncements that will give them a maximum security for all, that freedom, peace and justice which the common man of all, always desires.

So, while we were pursuing our military training in Tanzania, we were very much aware of this entrenched position of the Baganda which calls for a new Constitution for Uganda that will satisfy the basic aspirations of the Baganda. But, on the other hand, the fact also remains that those who demand a Federal Constitution are people who lacked adequate share of the national cake. Since the birth of Uganda, the Baganda lacked nothing of the sort. Everything which matters in terms of development is based in Buganda. In other words, as one Mr Roland Kakooza Mutale[130] put it once, that Uganda is '...Buganda...'! The demand by Baganda for Federal Constitution is tantamount to excessive greed.

As collaborators in the colonial enterprise, the Baganda fought side by side with the British to conquer and bring Bunyoro Kingdom under colonial rule with considerable loss of lives. For this collaboration, the British gave Buganda six counties of Bunyoro as war spoils, thus expanding the boundaries of Buganda Kingdom considerably. Buganda Kingdom therefore gained its present size after getting six counties from defeated Bunyoro Kingdom. Why was Buganda hurt by the loss of the two counties of '...*Buyaga*...' and '...*Bugangaizi*...' to Bunyoro Kingdom? Yet this was what was agreed by all parties at the Lancaster House,

---

[130] By 1979-80 was a journalist/Editor of The Economy & Mulengera Newspapers but took up arms in 1981 under National Resistance Army (NRA) to remove the Dr Obote government. Now retired at a military rank of Major but remains a Presidential Adviser on Political Affairs.

London, in the last independence conference to the 1962 Independence Agreement that the matter should be settled.

The reaction of the President of Uganda, Sir Edward Mutesa-II on the outcome of the referendum by refusing to sign the instrument for transferring the '...*lost counties...*' into law was uncalled for. His refusal to sign the instrument was tantamount to suspension and abrogation of the 1962 semi-federal Constitution. For the sake of peace, security and harmony the Kabaka and the Baganda could have accepted the outcome of the 1964 referendum. All along, the spirit which Baganda have demonstrated has been of their point of view and personal advantage or gain; it was not a patriotic spirit.

In 1875, when Mutesa-I sent Henry Morton Stanley[131] to Queen Victoria, and invited missionaries to come and educated his subjects he did not realise, up to the time of his death on 9th October 1884, that he, (Mutesa-1, that is) had started an evolution of a revolution which would spread beyond the borders of his Kingdom.

In essence, by doing this Mutesa-I was asking for change and once change had come, Baganda should agree to abide by it. Kabaka Mwanga of Buganda Kingdom understood this fact very well when he found himself being led together with Omukama Kabalega of Bunyoro Kingdom into exile to the Seychelles Island.

As far as we fighters of Save Uganda Movement (SUM) were concerned, It dawned on us therefore that we had no option but we had to learn to live with a brother however greedy he may be because he was our brother. For the sake of avoiding further blood-spilling, destruction of property and loss of valuable time for economic development of Uganda we must go back and agree willingly to make a new arrangement based on a Federal Constitution that will enable us to live in peace, security and harmony. Even though this was our position, we left this issue

---

[131] Explore/journalist associated with the historical quote '...*Dr Livingstone I presume...*'

for discussion by all Ugandans of goodwill until an amicable solution could be reached after the ousting of Idi Amin-Dada from power.

With the elimination of the Mutesa-II/Ibingira/Opolot faction, the Idi Amin-Dada faction and Dr Apollo Milton Obote faction came into sharper focus. We saw that from 1966 up to 1971 the politics of factionalism continued unabated in Uganda and the two factions, have been contending for power such that any keen observer of Uganda's political scene could clearly see.

Notes 2.

To answer this question, we realised that towards Uganda's independence from Britain, there were many junior officers in the Kings African Rifles (KAR)[132] who were promoted to their various ranks on the basis of seniority in the army. Such semi-literate Junior Officers in Uganda Army who were promoted, in our view, had reached their ceiling. They did not deserve to be promoted any further when 'KAR' became Uganda Army once Uganda attained independence. They did not deserve to be over promoted up to a level of senior military officers because they lacked basic schooling that was required.

The only credit Idi Amin-Dada and the likes like him had was seniority. Idi Amin-Dada was educated up to primary four and/or there about. He learnt military skills on the job for which he earned promotion up to junior officer level. He did not go through any military academy and any war college. He spoke English with a lot of difficulty. How could he be promoted up to the level of Army Commander of a country? He did not deserve to walk in the corridor of power of any country. Those who should be delegated the responsibilities to walk in any corridor of

---

[132] Ibid 70.

power should be those who could lead a country in any eventuality.

On 23rd January 1964, there was an Army Mutiny over conditions of service and Africanisation in all three independent counties of East Africa.

In Uganda, the Minister of State for Internal affairs, Mr Felix Onama was taken hostage for 24 hours at Jinja Military Barracks. Prime Minister, Dr Apollo Milton Obote requested for British military troops which were flown in from Kenya to quell the mutiny. The government subsequently increased army salaries and replaced Col. R. Groome[133] with a Ugandan Col. Shaban Opolot as Army Commander of the replacement Uganda Army.

It was the way Prime Minister Dr Apollo Milton Obote handled this mutiny which eventually led into Idi Amin-Dada ascending onto power in Uganda. The Prime Minister, Dr Apollo Milton Obote, just went ahead to promote many semi-literate junior officers into senior level. This was a source of calamity, possible catastrophe for us all because it gave the power of the gun into the hands of ignorant, treacherous and brutal leaders like Idi Amin-Dada and their bed-fellows, whenever there would be any civil commotion or otherwise in Uganda. These semi-literate junior officers were over-promoted ostensibly to answer the call for Africanisation in the officer corps of the Uganda Army.

But Africanisation in the Uganda army should not have been effected on the stroke of a pen like that. Africanisation of the officer corps of Uganda Army was supposed to take its natural course when the military personnel go through military academies and then to war college to attain levels of senior military officers. This was the mistake that Prime Minister Dr Apollo Milton Obote and his associates made which led to the problem Ugandans found themselves in, in 1977. A problem

---

[133] Military commander of the Uganda arm of the Kings African Rifles (KAR) - 1956-62.

which we were trying to solve by embarking on the armed struggle against Idi Amin-Dada and his regime.

Dr Apollo Milton Obote could have saved Uganda from this peril if only he had commissioned and promoted to senior levels only educated junior officers, and they were fairly many in the Uganda Army then. Africanisation in the officer corps was an aspiration which all Ugandans aspired to which was why they asked for independence from Britain in 1962. Africanisation of the officer corps of Uganda was not something that could take place immediately in 1964 as the Uganda Army was demanding for in their mutiny. In the true sense, Africanisation of the officer corps of Uganda Army required recruitment of suitably qualified Ugandan youths as officer cadets to undergo military training through military academy and later war college abroad.

With promotion of semi-literate junior officers up to senior military officer ranks, the Prime Minister of Uganda, Dr. Apollo Milton Obote possibly thought that he was guarding his regime against military *coup d'état*, which was rampant then in newly independent countries, with highly educated officer corps personnel. Dr Apollo Milton Obote used to boast that he was among those African leaders who did not fear coups. Yet it is now history that in Uganda, a semi-literate senior military officer overthrew Dr Apollo Milton Obote's government regardless of his lack of competence to lead a country.

Dr Apollo Milton Obote perhaps thought that these poorly educated senior military officers in Uganda Army would lack ambition to stage a *coup d'état*. But it seems ambition is something that both poorly educated, and highly educated individuals harbour regardless of their lack of competence to lead a country.

And, it was indeed shameful to see Idi Amin-Dada ascend to the Presidency of Uganda without even the knowledge of any workable English or communication. But if Dr. Apollo Milton Obote had exercised due diligence and vigilance, by stopping Idi

Amin-Dada from walking in the corridors of power in Uganda, he could have saved Uganda from the embarrassment Uganda found herself in.

The kind of atrocities Idi Amin-Dada and his bed-fellows meted on the people of Uganda were acts of semi-literate, ignorant, and treacherous and brutal persons who did not deserve in any way to lead any country in this modern era of democracy. This was the case because Idi Amin-Dada lacked the basics of statesmanship.

Upon attainment of the Presidency of Uganda, Idi Amin-Dada copied the example set by his predecessor, Dr Apollo Milton Obote. He promoted illiterate and semi-literate Nubians and Kakwa in Uganda Army up to any level of officer corps. By doing this, the power of the gun in Uganda was firmly established in the hands of ignorant, semi-literate senior military officers who abused the use of such power at will doing whatever civil commotion there was or otherwise during the Idi Amin-Dada's regime.

However, to answer the same calls in the army mutiny of Tanganyika Army on the same date, 23rd January 1964, the President of Tanganyika, Mwalimu Julius Kambarage Nyerere sent home those semi-literate junior officers in the Tanganyika Army who were calling for Africanisation. President Nyerere could see very clearly that Africanisation of the officer corps of Tanganyika Army could not take place in 1964 as was being demanded by semi-illiterate junior officers. Mwalimu Nyerere appealed to members of his political party, the Tanganyika African National Union [TANU][134] at the grassroots all over Tanganyika to give him suitably qualifies youths to join Tanganyika Army as officer cadets. This they did, and they were sent abroad to military

---

[134] Political party name 1954-1977 that ended following a merger of TANU and Afro-Shirazi Party of Zanzibar. The result of the political union between Tanganyika and Zanzibar, resulted in the changed name of Chama Cha Mapinduzi (CCM).

academies in some commonwealth countries and elsewhere. After spending four years in military academies abroad they came back to Tanganyika and were given accelerated promotions to fill the vacuum left by whites who left Tanganyika Army when Tanganyika attained independence. Some of them who excelled during their training in military academies proceeded to war colleges abroad only to come back later to Tanganyika to fill the vacuum of senior military officers in the officer corps.

Mwalimu Julius Kambarage Nyerere did not promote semi-literate junior officers to satisfy the call for Africanisation in the 1964 army mutiny. If anything, he borrowed senior army officers from Nigeria to fill the vacuum left by the departure of white officers when Tanganyika attained independence to man the Tanganyika Army until such a time when Tanganyika got her own suitably qualifies and well-trained senior military officers.

Mwalimu Julius Kambarage Nyerere did this in good faith with great love for his country to ensure that the power of the gun did not fall into the hands of those who could abuse the use of such power whenever there is civil commotion or otherwise in Tanganyika. This made it possible for Tanganyika to enjoy continued peace, security and harmony since it attained her independence. Tanganyika later went ahead to unite with Zanzibar to become Tanzania. And one of the ingredients which enabled Tanzania to enjoy continued peace, security, and harmony has been the establishment of the power of the gun in the hands of educated, well-trained, and disciplined officers' corps of Tanzania Peoples Defence Forces [TPDF].

We could see how we fighters of Save Uganda Movement [SUM] and Uganda as a whole were going to benefit from the guidance and military skills these educated well-trained disciplined TPDF officers were going to equip us well to make it possible to oust Idi Amin-Dada from power.

Notes 3.

According to very reliable information we got from one of our military officer, Mr Apollo Ejou[135], this came about because Dr Apollo Milton Obote did not take the requisite urgent and vital decision to arrest, detain, and try Col. Idi Amin-Dada in a court of law.

Mr Apollo Ejou told us that from 1966 up to 1971, it was an open secret that Idi Amin-Dada was preparing a coup against Dr Apollo Milton Obote's government. He told us that the **General Service Unit (GSU)** gathered accurate intelligence information in this regard with concrete evidence and sent all this to the President, to cause the arrest of Col. Idi Amin-Dada. However urgent this was, critical decision was not forthcoming from the President.

In view of the weight of the information gathered about the preparation of the coup by Idi Amin-Dada, Dr Apollo Milton Obote should not have left for Singapore Commonwealth Heads of State Summit without ordering for the arrest of Col. Idi Amin-Dada and seeing to it that Idi Amin-Dada was effectively behind bars ready for prosecution in a court of law. However, in this respect, the President of Uganda, Dr Apollo Milton Obote, we were told, disappointed everybody. He did this by delegating the arrest of Idi Amin-Dada into the hands of his trusted senior security officers. When he was leaving for Singapore, he told them that when he came back, he wanted to find Col Idi Amin-Dada behind bars.

However, what Idi Amin-Dada did was to outwit Dr Apollo Milton Obote's trusted senior security officers by rescheduling the D-day for his coup before he was arrested. By doing this, Idi Amin-Dada carried the day. We therefore took note of the fact that we were suffering because of the negligence of Dr Apollo

---

[135] Ibid 29.

Milton Obote. He did not do what was expected of him as the President of a country and should not vie again to regain power in Uganda, if only to repeat the same mistakes again.

Notes 4.

> On 13th February 1971, Col. Idi Amin-Dada was sworn in as President of Uganda.

We saw that fascist dictatorship was a brand-new phenomenon in Uganda such that Ugandans could not fully understand its working and how best to counter react against it. As a consequence, most Ugandans did not know how to react against it in order to regain their freedom. Many believed that it was the Almighty God who put him there and it was up to the Almighty God to remove him from power. This attitude was a blessing which enabled Idi Amin-Dada to cling to power for 8 years.

Peasants in Uganda responded to the fascist dictatorship by returning to subsistence production, while civil servants adopted a 'do-not-care' attitude. The religious leaders on the other hand could at times pluck courage and denounce brutalities and excesses. But such passive resistance only affected the regime marginally and therefore a blessing too to Idi Amin-Dada.

Political tyranny and militarised social order became so pervasive such that even opposition to the regime both inside and outside Uganda became largely disorganised, disunited and sectarian all to the advantage of Idi Amin-Dada and his cronies. Idi Amin-Dada suppressed brutally any internal political and military resistance to his regime. This instilled a lot of fear in the hearts of Ugandans.

Externally based opposition and resistance to the Idi Amin-Dada's regime by Ugandans exiles were largely divided and disorganised. Scattered all over the world, but mainly concentrated in neighbouring states of eastern and central Africa, the opposition could hardly establish a platform of compromise to organise a force that could oust Idi Amin-Dada. Ideological, organisational and leadership wrangles featured more permanently in the opposition as the nature and consequences of fascism at home.

As a result, external opposition ranged from humble welfare groups supporting refugees and exiles in matters of survival like the late Bishop Festo Kivengyere's[136] Relief Education Training Uganda Refugees Now [RETURN]; human rights and action groups such as Uganda Human Rights Group [UHRG] in Nairobi, to armed groups bent on removing Idi Amin-Dada by whatever means.

The armed groups ranged against Idi Amin-Dada included even mercenaries-oriented groups as the Popular Front for the Liberation of Uganda [PFLU] led by the late Mr John Odong'kara – a former Uganda Special Forces Police Commandant, whose mission was to use Israel in the removal of Idi Amin-Dada with American support; the Uganda Society [US] of Dr Martin Aliker[137], and; Prof Yusuf Kironde-Lule[138] - employing the same tactic as PFLU; and the Uganda National Organisation [UNO] whose '...Equatorial Brigade...' of 200-300 commandos led by Col. Bolka Bar-Levi[139] was meant to liberate Uganda in 1978 with the support of Mr Robert Mukasa, Mr Robert Serumaga[140] and Mr Andrew Adimola[141].

---

[136] First Anglican Bishop of Kigezi and exiled from 1977 after death of Archbishop Luwum – see Ibid 13, 14, 15.
[137] Dentist and Senior Political Adviser to President Museveni since 1986
[138] Ex-Chancellor Makerere University 1964-1970; President of Uganda 1979 (for 68 days) under Uganda National Liberation Front (UNLF); recalled by the ancestors in 1985
[139] Of Israeli Intelligence.
[140] Playwriter associated with Uganda National Cultural Centre; then under Uganda National Liberation Front (UNLF) 1979 became Minister of Commerce (for 68 days); recalled by the ancestors in 1980.
[141] First Uganda Ambassador to the Court of St James 1960; Permanent

These brief-case armed groups who were bent at removing Idi Amin-Dada from power by whatever military means possible were the '...*desperados*...' as far as we were concerned. We were of this view because they could not even see the string or in this case the rope that the mercenaries were going to attach with their help to hand Idi Amin-Dada. The mercenaries would no doubt set conditions that would undermine our sovereignty. Yet we had already gained our independence on 9th October 1962 from the British. Idi Amin-Dada's coup was a neo-colonial coup meant to retard economic development of Uganda. How on earth then could neo-colonialists prick their own eyes by removing Idi Amin-Dada from power and replace him with a new set of leaders however pro-Western they may be?

> On 4th July 1976, Israel's military commandos staged the famous Entebbe Raid to rescue their nationals being held hostage by Palestinians who had hijacked them on an Air France flight to Europe.

Why was it that the West did not turn the 'raid' into a coup against Idi Amin-Dada's regime? We fighters of SUM took this lack of action by Western powers to remove Idi Amin-Dada by whatever military means as a mockery on their part. Hoping in mercenaries to launch attacks to oust Idi Amin-Dada from power was not feasible as far as we were concerned.

In our view, even if such a venture came to reality, it would be costly to our country in the long-term. These Ugandan exiles who were harbouring the ides of liberating Uganda by the help of mercenaries had just formed imaginary 'road blocks' fighting groups meant to ambush any would be leader that was going to replace Idi Amin-Dada to accommodate them in his government on the ground that they also had fighting groups.

Secretary in various ministries; Minister for Reconstruction and Rehabilitation in 1979 under Uganda National Liberation Front (UNLF); later head of Uganda Cement Corporation; and Member of the Constituent Assembly that framed the NRA-regimes 1995 Constitution.

In our view, Uganda needed a credible opposition in the form of a front or a liberation movement that would recruit Uganda youths, train, and arm them to embark on armed struggle against Idi Amin-Dada's regime. Such credible armed opposition would be a platform of compromise that would bring all interest groups ranged against Idi Amin-Dada under its wings to oust Idi Amin-Dada from power. Hence, any interest groups acting in opposition to oust Idi Amin-Dada from power in isolation from any national platform of compromise would not succeed.

In this respect, there were many attempts on the part of the industrial and agricultural work force to voice their opposition, like the famous Lugazi Sugar Works and Kinyala Sugar Estate strikes in 1974 and 1976. There were also massive protests and strikes at Kilembe Copper Mines in 1975 where leaders of the strikes were killed, and the workers union banned. The massive protests and strikes by these workers amounted to nothing in absence of an articulate political leadership, a big section of which was languishing in exile.

Hence, the struggle of the workers could not pose a serious challenge to the trigger-happy primitive force of Idi Amin-Dada, because they were not acting in support of any liberation movement.

Even when Makerere University students tried to organise against the regime in 1975 and 1976, the consequences were as brutal as expected, leading to imprisonment and death of some students because the students tried to organise against the military regime in isolation of any national liberation movement.

Within the armed forces, the opposition to the Idi Amin-Dada regime was largely a victim of sectional interest and the culture of a political force, inherited from the colonial days. The initial 1971-72 opposition was systematically eliminated as the regime ably exploited existing ethnic differences. To the surprise of many foreigners and Ugandans who could not understand the working of a fascist dictatorship, Idi Amin-Dada was able to survive numerous army-based attempted coup d'état, including the February 1974, Lt. Col. Ondoga[142] incidence and a coup attempt by Brig. Charles Arube in March 1974. The two were serious attempts by West Nilers[143] themselves to remove Idi Amin-Dada from power.

To eliminate any threat from within the army, Idi Amin-Dada carried out frequent purge of officers who appeared enlightened and militarily well-trained, especially those from other than Kakwa and Nubian tribes. The result was an ill-trained, illiterate, and semi-literate army who were ready to kill and torture in order to generate fear in the population. Fear instilled in the population, was a blessing which enabled Idi Amin-Dada to continue misruling Uganda.

In July 1976, a daring assassination attempt was made on Idi Amin-Dada after he had addressed policemen in Nsambya Police Training School. His driver was killed but Idi Amin-Dada escaped. The response of Gen. Mustafa Adrisi, Idi Amin-Dada's Vice President, to the assassination attempt was to warn all Ugandans that the death of Idi Amin-Dada could have led to Kampala being bathed in blood. Idi Amin-Dada was shortly thereafter made '...*Life President*...' according to the proposal of Ankole elders at some point.

Any credible opposition that could remove Idi Amin-Dada from power or pose a serious threat against him was in the form of a front or a liberation movement that would recruit, train and arm those trained to embark on armed struggle to oust Idi Amin-Dada from power as I had already indicated before.

---

[142] See Ibids 21 & 22
[143] Infers to the nationalities hailing from the District of West Nile, and home of Idi Amin-Dada. Published anecdotes suggest the fallout inferred to here was about non-indigenous military officers said to be of Sudanic origin were in control of the Army.

One of such credible opposition was that of Dr Apollo Milton Obote which appeared in September 1972 and invaded Uganda from Tanzania with the aim of enabling Dr Apollo Milton Obote to regain power in Uganda. Taking the advantage of the Asian expulsion and the foreign anti-Amin sentiment, Dr Apollo Milton Obote and Mr Yoweri Museveni[144] with tacit approval of the Tanzania government, launched their invasion with hurriedly assembled and ill-trained fighters through Masaka and Mbarara hoping to spark-off a mass uprising of the Uganda Peoples Congress (UPC) supporters.

This invasion which was based on assumption failed. After a brief engagement of the Idi Amin-Dada's troops in the dawn attack, the guerrillas were repulsed and others quickly surrounded and massacred in the Mbarara Simba Barracks. Suspected rebel sympathisers were publicly executed. Despite the intervention of church leaders and human rights organisations, Amin carried out the death sentences by firing squad in various towns in the name of teaching the opponents a lesson.

The September 1972 invasion of Uganda from Tanzania opened a new chapter of unprecedented murders and sadistic torture with people buried alive and others forced to eat their own private parts. The abortive invasion did not only give Amin a chance to kill anyone he regarded as a threat but it also provided him with propaganda ammunition against Julius Kambarage Nyerere[145], forcing Nyerere to sign a Mogadishu Agreement, brokered by Somali President Siad Barre[146], whose terms were to stop Tanzania from allowing its territory to be used by Tanzania exiles, to destabilise Idi Amin-Dada.

---

[144] Later leader of Front for National Salvation Army (FRONASA) - 1973-1980; Minister of Defence 1979-80 under the Uganda National Liberation Front (UNLF) government; President of Uganda from 1986-on under the National Resistance Army (NRA)-government.
[145] Ibid 1 & 6.
[146] Recalled by the ancestors 1995.

The defeat of the small contingent of guerrillas composed largely of former soldiers and Uganda Peoples Congress (UPC) supporters, was followed by widespread persecution of all those suspected to have been sympathetic to the invasion. May prominent UPC supporters especially in Mbarara and Bushenyi Districts were killed while many went to exile.

It is due to this ill-fated invasion and its aftermath that a number of exiles parted company with Dr Apollo Milton Obote to form their own fighting groups. To the best of our knowledge not many credible fighting groups were formed, however. Mr Yoweri Museveni went ahead to form the **F**ront for **N**ational **S**alvation [FRONASA][147]. FRONASA modelled along the group FRELIMO[148] of Mozambique, attempted to base its programme in Uganda through underground recruitment and training fighters. These guerrillas were then infiltrated into Uganda to carryout various acts of sabotage.

Operating under the difficult Mogadishu Agreement terms, FRONASA was not able to provide any effective, anti-Amin armed opposition, especially in view of the numbers of cadres it kept losing to Idi Amin-Dada's secret agents inside Uganda.

And, without any reasonable doubt, **S**ave **U**ganda **M**ovement [SUM] was the third credible fighting group that had joined the fray. We have done this when the two credible fighting groups I have already mentioned had burnt their fingers and were inactive. Our hope was that, once we start our armed struggle against Idi Amin-Dada's regime, they would join us in this noble cause. SUM came into being as a result of a merger between two fighting groups; one that was formed by Ateker Ejalu[149] [RIP], and

---

[147] Founded in 1973; participated in Anti-Amin 1978-79 war that constructed the Uganda National Liberation Front (UNLF) government; and wound up in 1980.
[148] Founded in1962 and took political power in Mozambique 1975, that is, post-Portuguese colonial rule.
[149] Ibid 46.

that which was formed by Engineer Akena p'Ojok and his colleagues

Notes 5.

Mzee Otoa's son, Mr James Obua-Otoa was later appointed one of the Uganda National Liberation Front (UNLF)-government Minister after the fall of Idi Amin-Dada's regime. He was Minister of Tourism and Wildlife - 1979-1980; and thereafter Uganda's Ambassador to German 1980-1985 under the Uganda Peoples Congress (UPC) government.

Notes 6.

2nd Lt. Kenneth Kaunda Banya was '*KK*'[150], as we used to refer to him. With the help of those veterans liberated Kitgum before the arrival of liberators from Tanzania. Hence, on record that Kitgum therefore remained the only area in Uganda liberated from the hands of Idi Amin-Dada by its own people with the help of our organisation during the 1979 liberation war.

Notes 7.

This being the case, we succeeded immensely where the two fighting groups of Dr Milton Obote and Mr Yoweri Museveni ranged earlier on against Idi Amin-Dada's regime failed. And, it was our success against Idi Amin-Dada's regime which earned us the enmity of these two fighting groups against us. Yet we were fighting for the same cause. They could have looked at us ideal as ally in their struggle against Idi Amin-Dada but jealously took the better part of their hearts.

---

[150] See Flagpost 1. The 'KK' inference arose from the same as of then President of Zambia Kenneth Kaunda's 'KK'.

Notes 8.

At this juncture, it suffice for me to tell the world why Tanzania Peoples' Defence Forces (TPDF) invaded Uganda to the extent of overthrowing Idi Amin-Dada from power with the help of Ugandan fighting groups like Kikosi Maalum (KM), Front for National Salvation (FRONASA) and Save Uganda Movement (SUM). Some people up to this day think that it was Idi Amin-Dada's attempt to export his excesses to neighbouring countries that provoked an external reaction that toppled him. This assertion is true but not to the whole extent because political events take place only when they are planned.

It was truism that Tanzania was harbouring a lot of fear, of Idi Amin-Dada then, why? This fear had to do with Idi Amin-Dada, linking up with any political organisation led by a Moslem in Tanzania to cause mayhem that may be could lead to the overthrow of Tanzanian government then. This might have been a farfetched supposition, but it was feasible. Idi Amin-Dada's regime was a nuisance as far as Tanzania was concerned, then. But how best could Tanzania get rid of Amin? Tanzania had to get a viable ally from Uganda in order to do this. By 1978, there was no viable ally from Uganda that could help Tanzania to fight Idi Amin-Dada to the finish. It was only Save Uganda Movement [SUM] that fitted in the design of Tanzania to fight Idi Amin-Dada out of power.

So, **SUM** was delegated the honourable task of carrying out activities that may enable the Tanzania People Defence Forces (TPDF) to invade and fight Idi Amin-Dada out of power. This was the case because to invade Uganda and fight Idi Amin-Dada out of power, she must have viable reasons to tell the world.

I have stated already that the early infiltration of our combatants into Uganda, which was carried out by our leaders in Tanzania without the knowledge of those based in Kenya was a misadventure. It resulted into the arrest of three of our combatants[151]; namely Mr Charles Oburu, Mr David Kitara and Mr Gulu. This took place in early March 1978. They were badly tortured and taken before Idi Amin-Dada and revealed who they were and what their mission was. Form their utterances Idi Amin-Dada got to know what was afoot.

By September 1978, Idi Amin-Dada told the world that Tanzania had invaded Uganda. The world possibly, could not believe in the accusation. But the fact remained that Idi Amin-Dada had already arrested three of our combatants and extracted the fact from them. It was only good that none of us already knew the name of our organisation otherwise a lot of facts could have been revealed. I got to know the name of our organisation as Save Uganda Movement (SUM) some days before the D-day when we were brought our propaganda leaflets. Idi Amin-Dada had already known that and was then right in accusing Tanzania of invading Uganda.

Faced with these kinds of facts, Idi Amin-Dada decided to take the war to Tanzania. Idi Amin-Dada used to brag openly that the Swahilis cannot fight. With this biased opinion, he thought that he could take the war to Tanzania and do what he fancied without any backlash. This explains why Idi Amin-Dada intensified the movement of his troops towards the border with Tanzania and intensified attacks on Tanzania whom he accused of invading Uganda in September 1978. Hence;

> On 19th September 1978, Idi Amin-Dada's MiG jet fighters bombed Tanzania.
>
> On 9th October 1978, Idi Amin-Dada's troops crossed into Tanzania.
>
> On 12th October 1978, Amin accused Tanzania of invading Uganda.

---

[151] See Dedication & Flagpost 1

On 28th October 1978, Amin ordered bombing of Kyaka village and Bukoba Town (Tanzania) which were turned into ghost places.

On 4th November 1978: Kagera bridge was blown up by Idi Amin-Dada's' troops under the command of Lt. Col. Marijan and an orgy of looting, raping and killing started with properties and animals brought to Uganda along with schools girls.

On 5th November 1978, Idi Amin-Dada challenged Nyerere to a boxing fight, near the border.

On 14th November 1978, Tanzania massed troops near the border. Idi Amin-Dada claimed that the invasion had been repulsed with heavy casualties on the side of the invaders. On the same day meetings of anti-Amin groups in Dar es Salam and Nairobi became regular with little success on unity.

Notes 9.

With developments at the military front, time moved fast. We did not carry out any sabotage again until we were ordered to withdraw to Nairobi towards the fall of Kampala on 11th April 1979.

Notes 10.

Later on, Dr Milton Obote would use the catchy words:
'...*show me your commanders...*'

in his Presidential campaign of the 1980 general elections. He kept on telling Ugandans in his campaign that UPC is everywhere and all of us are UPC.

Notes 11.

To us in SUM, these two Airforce Officers Capt. David Omitta [RIP] and Capt. Sam Walugembe [RIP] were heroes whose war efforts against Idi Amin-Dada's Army should be very much appreciated and honoured. They did everything within their power to help in the war effort against Idi Amin-Dada.

Notes 12.

When Idi Amin-Dada's Regime was toppled, our leaders informed the Chief of Staff of Uganda National Liberation Army [UNLA], the late David Oyite Ojok[152] about the roles some officers and other ranks within Idi Amin-Dada's army did, but, Oyite Ojok could not accept that these officers and other ranks collaborated with us in the war effort against Idi Amin-Dada. Flight Engineer Jack Oita Alecho tried his level best to explain this matter to all who mattered in the Uganda National Liberation Army [UNLF] government to no avail. The Tanzania Peoples Defence Forces (TPDF) insiders knew the truth but did not intervene in the internal contradictions of the nascent Uganda National Liberation Army (UNLA).

It would be unfair if I do not mention the names of some political leaders of SUM who were in Uganda with whom I interacted a great deal during 1978-1979 war against Idi Amin-Dada. I dealt a great deal with Flight Engineer Jack Oita Alecho.

---

[152] Recalled by the ancestors in 1983

Remember, he was the one who was taking us from Nairobi to Namanga border post in his blue Alfa Romeo, when he was still working with the East African Airways (EAA). The liberation war against Idi Amin-Dada came into play when Flight Engineer Jack Oita Alecho was then based in Entebbe working with Uganda Airlines. With the demise of East African Community in July 1977, EAA was no more. Airmen who were Ugandan working with EAA went back to their respective countries to serve with their national airways created by their respective government of their countries.

Flight Engineer Jack Oita Alecho is an intelligent and quick-witted fellow from my point of view. As usual when he was in Nairobi, and now in Uganda, he pre-occupied himself when he was off-duty to help in the liberation war efforts. We used to call him '...7.30...' *but* have no idea how this code came about. He could feed us with any information that he deemed we ought to know and that he knew would be of help in the war efforts against Idi Amin-Dada. During the war he used to fly to Libya to ferry support weapons to Uganda which Idi Amin-Dada and Muammar al Qadhafi thought could be of help to turn the tide against Tanzania. When we were short of subsistence allowance Jack would give us money within his means.

I must mention here also Mr Odoi Chwalle[153], (SUM code name 'CJ'). He was a lawyer and a close associate of Mr Dennis Echwou. Odoi was working with the Uganda Judiciary as a State Attorney based in Gulu. The trios, Mr Dennis Echwou, Mr Odoi Chwalle, and Flight Engineer Jack Oita Alecho were very active in the war efforts against Idi Amin-Dada. In my estimation, the trios contributed more than their shares in that respect.

There was also a Mr Karamagi who had an office in National Insurance Corporation [NIC] building in Kampala. I went to meet him one day during the war to pick some monies for the war

---

[153] Ibid 104

efforts. He wanted to know whether I was one of the SUM guerrillas. I told him that I was one of them. Mr Karamagi was so scared that I was not supposed to know him. I assured him if any misfortune befalls me, I will not mention him to anybody.

Eng. Leo Obonyo, a Fellow of Royal Electronic Engineer (FREE) was also our active member. He was then the Training Officer with Uganda Broadcasting Corporation. He too contributed a lot with giving/passing to us information we required for the war. I cannot mention all the names of all those who hosted us at their homes in Jinja and Kampala before and during the war against Idi Amin-Dada's regime[154].

But it would be unfair if I do not mention the names of heroines of the war, namely, Ms Jeroline Apio and Ms Rachael Ayaa. I have already mentioned them earlier on. The two played the crucial role of hosting us and collecting military information from military officers, they knew which helped a great deal in the war:

- Ms Jeroline Apio was a saleswoman in the shop of one Idi Amin-Dada's military officer in Luwum Street in Kampala. She usually picked and told us any crucial information she gathered from Idi Amin-Dada's senior military officers whenever they were coming from the war front, whenever they called in the shop of their colleague. Without exception, many of them were sad and doubted whether they were going to win the war. They normally wore sad faces and doubted a great deal, whether they would win the war against the Tanzania Peoples Defence Force (TPDF) and their Ugandan fighting groups. Most of them, if anything were concerned about sending members of their families' home or outside the country. These pieces of information gathered by Ms Jeroline Apio boosted our morale a great deal.

---

[154] See Flagpost 4 SUM Operational Theatre.

- Ms Rachael Ayaa on the other hand was working with Uganda Blankets Manufacturers on Old Portbell Road. She too did her best in gathering intelligence information from military officers she knew. It was difficult for us to tell who was out performing who in gathering intelligence information from the two heroines.
- 'Ms CK' - whose full names I do not remember was a lady resident at the Young Women's Christian Association (YWCA) hostel - 1978-79, in Kampala. She was introduced to us by Flight Engineer Jack Oita Alecho. This '...CK[155] lady...' kept in storage the most important and valuable cargo that we eventually used to start the sabotage activities in and around Kampala[156]. It was these activities that signalled the counter offensive by the Tanzania Peoples Defence Force (TPDF) against the Idi Amin-Dada-Regime.

I must also mention the contribution of our communication men: Mzee Otoa based in Jinja and my brother Mr John Okoya based in Kampala. The two by coincidence were Kings African Rifles [KAR][157] veterans who served as signallers during their active service. By the time of 1978-1979 liberation war against Idi Amin-Dada both were working as telephone operators at their respective work places. Mzee Otoa was then a telephone operator with British American Tobacco Ltd [BAT] at Jinja. My elder brother Mr John Okoya, on the other hand was a telephone operator with McKenzie Technical Services Ltd on Nasser Road in Kampala. The two gave us information from our leaders based in Nairobi and gave them updates of the war in Uganda.

Last but not least, I must mention the contribution of one Mr Ojege and one Mr Oyoo who were based in Jinja working with National Water and Sewerage Corporation. Each of them hosted more than two of our fighters. I do not know how I should thank

---

[155] God willing, she consents that her name can be revealed.
[156] See Notes 8.
[157] Ibid 70.

all those gallant sons and daughters of Uganda who hosted out fighters. They deserve great appreciation and rewards. It is very unfortunate that they did not gain anything in the form of rewards from leaders of SUM for the patriotic duties they performed. I lack words I should use to thank them. May the Almighty God bless them in everything they did and everything they will do in their life time.

Notes 13.

First among them are a group of Makerere University graduates who were intimate friends of Mr Dennis Echwou:
- Mr Odoi Chwalle, a lawyer who graduated together with Dennis Echwou. Then as a Judge, Mr Odoi Chwalle was working as State Attorney based in Gulu.
- Mr Silver Gidongo, a social scientists who graduated from Makerere University with Mr Dennis Echwou. Then was working with Coffee Marketing Board as Principal Human Resources Personnel. He had an office in Amber House, Kampala.
- Mr Elias Wanyama, telecommunication technician, then working with Uganda Posts and Telecommunication in Telephone House, Kampala.

Mr Dennis Echwou, Mr Odoi Chwalle, Flight Engineer Jack Oita Alecho, Mr Silver Gidongo and Mr Elias Wanyama were very active in the war efforts against Idi Amin-Dada in 1978-1978. In my estimation, and from where I was standing while engaging with them, these gallant sons of Uganda contributed more than their fair share in the liberation war.

Notes 14

At the State Research Bureau (SRB) in Nakasero, they were badly tortured and the person who arrested them told them that he was still thinking how he should kill them but will come the next morning to kill them. They were arrested because one of my nephews who was a Police Officer accused them when an SRB officer arrested him over some trivial matter. Mr John Okoya and his colleagues showed us their blood-stained dresses. But they were saved because Kampala was liberated the very night they were arrested. There were some SRB personnel who were also detained because of indiscipline. They did not want to go to the front line, hence they were detained. They were mainly Tutsi refugees[158]. They sensed that Kampala was already liberated. They tied their bed sheets together and used them as a rope to descend from the floor their cell was situated through the window up to the ground.

Mr John Okoya and his colleagues seized the opportunity to escape from Nakasero by using the bed sheets tied together by day break. On reaching the streets, they oriented themselves towards Nakawa Estate. As they walked along the street towards the Estate, they met some liberators who stopped them and demanded to know who they were. They informed the liberators that they were detainees who had just escaped from State Research Bureau Headquarters (SRB) at Nakasero. The liberators sympathised with them and left them to proceed where they were going.

They had hardly departed from the company of the liberators when one of Idi Amin-Dada's soldiers appeared riding a brand-new bicycle. He was wondering aloud that surely the liberators had captured Kampala. John and his colleagues drew the attention of the liberators about the lone soldier of Idi Amin-

---

[158] Infers to those nationalities hailing from the neighbouring countries of either Rwanda or Burundi seeking safety in Uganda because of civil strife in those respective countries. Uganda not only accommodated them but also supported in both meaningful and gainful living, hence finding roles in Intelligence/security organs.

Dada. The liberators just shot him dead. They gave the bicycle the soldier was riding to Mr John Okoya as a gift.

As I have already stated, Nakasero's SRB was a place of no return. No one from Nakawa Estate expected Mr John Okoya and his colleagues to live once they were taken there. Nevertheless Mr John Okoya and his colleagues appeared at Nakawa Estate all of a sudden.

Upon seeing Mr John Okoya and his colleagues, one Mzee George, an Acholi elder from Kitgum who was an ex-serviceman of Second World War was running away from him because he was not the one who had killed him. He thought this was an apparition. But Mr John Okoya assured Mzee George that he was the one, a real human being not a ghost.

Mr John Okoya went on to tell all the curious on-lookers that the Almighty God set them free from the SRB at Nakasero so let his name be praised!

Having ascertained the truth, Mzee George then sat cross legged and took off his shoes. He asked Mr John Okoya to come and sit cross-legged in front of him. He then took one of his shoes and hit the ground three times. He blessed Mr John Okoya, in a traditional Acholi way by spitting saliva on his chest and prayed that he must live till old age and must die in a sleep, peacefully.

The curious on lookers from Nakawa Estate escorted Mr John Okoya and his colleagues to Q10[159] where they welcomed them warmly and thanked the Almighty God for saving their lives. All the tenants who knew Mr John Okoya came one and came all to greet him and thank God. Everybody was in a mood of celebration with the departure of Idi Amin-Dada from power and the escape of Mr John Okoya and his colleagues from the notorious **State Research Bureau (SRB) Headquarter**.

---

[159] Ibid 59

When the celebration died out our combatants Mr Oketch Ojukwu armed himself with Makarov Pistol with enough ammunitions, took the new bicycle, which was given to Mr John Okoya as a gift and headed to Nsambya Police Barracks. Mr John Okoya told him not to go anywhere since the Almighty God has liberated them from hell itself! But Mr Oketch Ojukwu refused to take heed, he wanted to go and tell friends and relatives who were policemen that he was telling them the truth that Idi Amin-Dada will be toppled.

We learnt later that when he reached Nsambya Barracks he told his relatives that he told them the truth about the fall of Amin. His relatives did not want to hear such remark and shot him dead. Mr Oketch Ojukwu, an Acholi Labwor, was the only combatant who died from the combatants under my command. All the same, he did not die because of my fault! How I wished he had listened to my brother's advice.

Notes 15.

Noted loud absences in the rendezvous were those of our hosts and hostesses in Uganda who had the courage of harbouring us in their houses during the trying period of Idi Amin-Dada's regime at the peril of their lives. Time and space could not allow them to come and grace the occasion with their presence. They came later individually in groups to meet our leaders at their earliest convenience.

Notes 16.

So, our dear comrade Mr John Okumu Samora is resting in peace somewhere on Mengo Hill.

Mr John Okumu Samora was a brother-in-law of Mr David Kitara, remember, one of our three combatants who were arrested, detained and tortured by State Research Bureau (SRB) personnel and taken to Idi Amin-Dada Later on the three were executed. How we pray to Almighty God to rest the souls of our fallen combatants in eternal peace!

Notes 17.

Nothing came of Chief of Staff Lt. Col. David Oyite Ojok's promise. We remained operating at our own gathering intelligence information for our leaders as if we have not yet established a united front of compromise in the form of UNLF.

Much as Lt. Col. David Oyite Ojok did not co-opt us in his intelligence unit we had very little to complain so much about.

Notes 18.

Later, we learnt that his death had to do with fear of accountability of money which the Tanzania Government was giving SUM for carrying out its work. Mr William Ekweru knew a lot about how this money was mismanaged. Those who squandered the money developed a lot of fear that Tanzania government may ask for accountability of the money. To stop him from spilling the bean they had to silence him for ever by killing him. William Ekweru was killed by the Tanzanian and Uganda liberators. No one was arrested and prosecuted for his death. Here we are seeing a situation whereby the mother hen was eating some of the eggs she had layed! How hurt we were about the death of Mr William Ekweru.

Afterword 1:

HOW HAS THE MIGHTY FALLEN?

Several factors contributed to the fall of Idi Amin-Dada from power. The collapse of the economy during his rule was one of such factors. If opposition against his rule was no threat to his rule, the performance of the economy was. Production dwindled in all sectors of the economy and there was widespread shortage of nearly everything from sugar to petrol. Food became expensive and the population resorted to drinking crude '...*waragi*...' (war gins) - Uganda distilled spirits, as the shortage of beer continued to bite.

Factories and shops grabbed from Asians and allocated to Idi Amin-Dada's supporters were run down as most shoppers turned to Kenya and Sudan for even the most basic items. I recall that my cousin brother used to ride to South Sudan with Uganda produce to barter it for soap which he used to smuggle to Uganda to serve the need of our people.

Such was the scarcity of essential commodities in Uganda that one needed a chit from a Minister, a Senior Army Officer or a Provincial Governor in order to buy items like sugar, cooking oil and in many cases petrol. This legacy even went on during the Uganda National Liberation Front (UNLF)-era when Idi Amin-Dada was no longer in power. Allocation chits used to be ready cash for any essential commodity.

Even the boom from Coffee earnings in 1976-77 did not help to bring goods in the shops. If anything, it was Kenya that benefited a lot out of the so-called Coffee boom since most of Uganda coffee was smuggled there to fetch more money to the

coffee producers and middlemen from Uganda. Instead senior security officers and few trusted civil servants were allocated expensive vehicles to carry their favours while expensive suits and shirts from London were imported to be distributed to the army from their army shops cheaply to make the army happy.

As the economy gradually collapsed with production declining and the distribution network completely eroded the regime embarked on the use of stick and carrot tactics. Intensified civilian opposition were promised democracy in the form of Uganda National Forum (UNF), a body of hand-picked delegated who were supposed to advise the cabinet and the Defence Council (President Idi Amin-Dada himself in the real sense) about social, economic and political polices. The regime promised commissions of inquiry to investigate the abuse of human rights in response to mounting external condemnation. But, how could the so-called Commission of Inquiry investigate on reality? Promised Commission of Inquiry was meant to stonewall the issue of the abuse of human rights. In practice, there was an increase in murders, sackings, and retirements of prominent Ugandan both in public and military services.

With the economy becoming more chaotic, Idi Amin-Dada's new friends moved in. Arab countries moved in more strongly to provide necessary cash from oil money for the purchase of essential commodities and spare parts mainly for the army shops and the army respectively.

We may recall that Idi Amin-Dada's expulsion of the Israelis from Uganda on 23rd March 1972 was reciprocated with a visit by King Faisal of Saudi Arabia above all who offered a golden sword to Idi Amin-Dada as a weapon with which to Islamise Uganda, while Muammar al-Qaddafi called Idi Amin-Dada a '...*prophet of Islam...*'

A shrewd campaign in Islamic countries in Africa helped Idi Amin-Dada to pull a diplomatic coup by hosting the Organisation of African Unity (OAU) Heads of State Summit in Kampala. The holding of the summit had been strongly opposed by a number of African countries over Idi Amin-Dada's bad human rights record.

Nevertheless, Idi Amin-Dada became OAU Chairman 1975/76, Saudi Arabia, Kuwait and Libya sponsored the conference through a loan totalling shs 500 million. During the OAU summit, 4 British businessmen carried Idi Amin-Dada shoulder high, as Idi Amin-Dada demonstrated the '...*white man's burden*...'[160]

These achievements were however cosmetic and Idi Amin-Dada's international isolation gained momentum while local sentiments to his regime intensified leading to his downfall. The collapse of the economy was a serious issue since it had to do with putting food on the table at the end of the day. Ugandans were yearning for a better economy in which ends could meet. Hence, due to the prevailing state of the economy then, most Ugandans definitely wanted to see the back of Idi Amin-Dada but only that they lacked the power to do so. This explains why Ugandans warmly welcomed their liberators in 1979 to the extent of showering them with flowers wherever they went. Many Ugandans even volunteered to join the liberation army because they wanted a better economy.

Idi Amin-Dada was also someone who lived according to the famous adage that '...*there is no permanent friendship and enmity in politics*...'

> On 6th February 1971, we recall and remember that after his successful *coup d'état,* there were major celebrations held at Nakivubo Stadium.

British and Israeli diplomats were prominently catered for. No wonder, Israel and other Western counties were later implicated in the military coup that brought Idi Amin-Dada to power.

But, the honeymoon of this cordial diplomatic relationship between Idi Amin-Dada's government and the western countries

---

[160] now made famous by a Hollywood Film '...*The Last King of Scotland*...'

did not last for the whole of Idi Amin-Dada's tenure of power in Uganda much as the west might have put him there.

In July 1971, Idi Amin-Dada visited Israel and Britain in search of military aid. Britain agreed to supply equipment worth £1m (One Million Pounds Sterling) and to train personnel.

This military aid to Idi Amin-Dada got from Britain, seemed to have fallen short of his expectation. Upon his return from these visits, Idi Amin-Dada opted to forsake the cordial diplomatic relationship with the West even if they had assisted him to gain power. This measure of course led to Idi Amin-Dada's government international isolation later, but he cared less.

On 7th October 1971, Idi Amin-Dada embarked on causing trouble for the British Government and people. Idi Amin-Dada ordered a census of Asians in Uganda.

On 7th December 1971, Idi Amin-Dada cancels more than 12,000 applications by Asians for Ugandan citizenship.

On 8th December 1971, Idi Amin-Dada accused the Asians of sabotage and orders them to identify themselves with the African interests.

On 5th January 1972, he warned 15 Asian's representatives that Uganda is not an Indian country.

In February 1972, Idi Amin-Dada visited Libya and an agreement setting up Libyan-Arab Uganda Bank for Foreign Trade and Development holding 51% share capital of Ugshs 600 million was concluded. A Libyan military delegation then visited Uganda and promised '...every *assistance to the Uganda Army...*'

Save Uganda Movement [SUM]

It seemed Idi Amin-Dada had found what he wanted. Hence, from here onwards he diplomatically began to live by his famous '...*supersonic speed...*' adage. Idi Amin-Dada moved fast to drop diplomatic relations with Israel.

> On 23rd March 1972, Idi Amin-Dada informed the Israeli Ambassador that all Israelis would have to leave Ugandan soil in 4 days.

As a consequence;

> On 30th March 1972, the Israel Embassy was ordered to close and that was it with Israel.

> In April 1972 Britain sent a Military Training Team led by Lt Col Rogers [a former Idi Amin-Dada's Commanding Officer in Kings African Rifles (KAR)[161]] to replace Israeli Military Training Team.

Upon breaking diplomatic relations with Israel, Idi Amin-Dada now embarked on courting the friendship of the then Union of Soviet Socialist Republics (USSR).

> In July 1972, Idi Amin-Dada sent a 30-member military Uganda delegation headed by Acting Army Commander Col. Francis Nyangweso[162], comprising of at least 5 (five) Lt. Colonels, and a dozen military Majors, to visit USSR and secured substantial military aid. So far so good.

---

[161] Ibid 70
[162] Sports career as light heavyweight boxing champion from 1951 to 1962; Chairman of the National Council of Sports (NCS); Captain of the Ugandan boxing team from 1958 to Independence year 1962; winner for Uganda a boxing Bronze Medal at the 1962 Commonwealth Games at Perth. Presidency of Uganda Olympic Committee (UOC) for a staggering 29 years. Rose to rank of Major General and Chief of Staff in the Ugandan army, served as Defence Minister, plus Minister of Culture and Community Development in Amin-Dada's government. Recalled by the ancestors in 2012.

In August 1972 Idi Amin-Dada begins scaling down diplomatic relationship with Britain, that above all, was our former colonial master who introduced us in the modern world. Britain could have been a country that could maintain a cordial relationship with Uganda all the time. But in the esteem of Idi Amin-Dada Dada, this was not to be.

While addressing troops in the Tororo Town barracks;

On 4th August 1972, Idi Amin-Dada requested Britain to assume responsibility for British Asian citizens in Uganda.

On 5th August, a three-moth deadline was given to non-Uganda Asians of British origin to leave Uganda.

On 9thAugust 1972, Idi Amin-Dada extended expulsions to the Asians of Indian, Pakistani and Bangladeshi origins.

Campaign for Ugandanisation of commerce and industry began in earnest led by Mr Sam Ssebagereka[163] and Mr Joseph Mubiru[164], then Governor of Bank of Uganda. Government announces exemptions to professional Asians but these measures were revoked within a week. **Ugandan African Traders Associations (UATA) hold a public rally to support Asians total domination of Commerce and Industry in Uganda even though Uganda was now an independent country.** They were yearning for Africanisation of commerce and industry.

In September 1972, Idi Amin-Dada requests Libya for massive military aid.

---

[163] Served as Finance Minister in the Uganda National Liberation Front (UNLF) government 1979. Recalled by the ancestors in 1994.
[164] Murdered at the same time as Mr Benedicto Kiwanuka; Ibid 20.

On the 17th September, 1972, an invasion by the Obote's and Mr Museveni's guerrillas is launched from Tanzania.

Areas of Mutukula, Kyotera, Kakuto, and Kalisizo are briefly captured. But the invasion aborts. Libya sent 5 Hercules Transport – C130 planes with 400 troops and armaments. Libya proved her friendship to Idi Amin-Dada beyond reasonable doubt that a friend in need is a friend indeed.

On September 1972, Mr Benedicto Kiwanuka[165], Chief Justice and President General the Democratic Party (DP) is dragged from his chambers at a time of the East African Court of Appeal session and murdered, a week after he made a ruling against Uganda Government in '...*writ of habeas corpus*...' brought by the British High Commission concerning one Mr Donald Steward then held in custody by the military.

People in Kampala ran helter skelter that day because of the arrest of Mr Benedicto Kiwanuka without even knowing why they were running. I was in Nakawa Estate that afternoon, I saw people running in all directions, but not even one could tell me why he or she was running. Later, on it was British Broadcasting Corporation (BBC) radio service that came with the true version of what took place in its newscast of the day.

On October 7th 1972, Mr Joshua Wanume-Kibedi, Uganda Minister of Foreign Affairs, on behalf of Uganda and Mr John Malecela, Tanzania Minister of Foreign Affairs on behalf of Tanzania sign a Mogadishu Agreement on non-aggression, non-interference, and non-engagement in hostility propaganda.

---

[165] Ibid 20

On 13th October 1972, Tanzania closes Uganda guerrillas training camps and resettles most of them near Tabora to grow tobacco.

In November 1972, Idi Amin-Dada ordered a census of missionaries before expelling some of them from Uganda. Most of these missionaries expelled were from Western Countries. Their expulsion might have eroded further cordial diplomatic relations with those countries of the West where they came from.

In December 1972, Britain cancelled all aid to Uganda and Idi Amin-Dada responded by nationalising 41 foreign-owned firms, including 15 British firms.

In January 1973, Muammar al-Qadhafi visited Uganda.

On 24th January 1973, there was public execution of 'guerrillas'.

On 25th January, during the second anniversary of the Idi Amin-Dada's coup, government announced the setting up of 20 corporations to run the departed Asians business. The same day Mr Yoweri Museveni too launched his Front for National Salvation [FRONASA][166] to start a guerrilla war against Idi Amin-Dada.

On 12th February 1973, there were more public executions of guerrillas mainly from FRONASA.

In the same month of February, the Uganda military delegation visited France and secured 60 Armoured Personnel Carriers [APC] and 12 Mirage fighter jets paid for by Libya.

In April 1973, United States announces its intention to stop all Aid to Uganda but maintained training of State Research Bureau (SRB) personnel.

---

[166] Ibid 116 & 151.

In May 1973, while attending OAU Summit in Addis Ababa, Idi Amin-Dada and Julius Kambarage Nyerere met face-to-face for the first time since the coup in Uganda and signed accord whereby Idi Amin-Dada demanded to have Dr Apollo Milton Obote evicted from Tanzania.

On 30th June 1973, the US halted all Aid projects in Uganda.

At some point, a Decree giving Military Police powers of arrest were enacted.

In September 1973, Idi Amin-Dada offered to send soldiers to fight in the Middle East, and offered himself as Vanguard Commander for the Liberation of Africa. Uganda Government expelled Marine Guards from US Embassy and US advised all its' citizens in Uganda to leave.

In November 1973, United States of America (USA) closes its Embassy in Uganda.

In February 1974, the Christian Science Monitor (English Version) reports that USSR supplied Uganda with a squadron of MiG-fighters through Somalia.

In June 1974, Idi Amin-Dada threatened to expel all British citizens from Uganda in 48 hours.

On 10th July 1975, British Foreign Secretary, Mr James Callaghan[167] bowed before Idi Amin-Dada seeking the release of a British citizen Mr Denis Hills who was facing Idi Amin-Dada's demonstration of the "...*white man's burden*..."[168].

---

[167] Later Prime Minister of the United Kingdom from 1976 to 1979 and Leader of the Labour Party from 1976 to 1980.
[168] Ibid 164

Up to here it seems Idi Amin-Dada was enjoying a great deal the way he was humiliating Great Britain.

During January 1976, Idi Amin-Dada and the Palestine Liberation Organisation (PLO) signed an agreement for technical, economic, and scientific cooperation. Idi Amin-Dada handed over to the Palestine Liberation Organisation (PLO) a certificate of allocation for about 5,150 acres of land.

On June 10, 1976, Idi Amin-Dada survived an assassination attempt near Nsambya Police Training School. This led to the arrest of two German employees of Achelis Ltd, including its' General Manager, Mr Mubiru, found dead a week later.

On 25th June 1976, Lt. Col. Godwin Sule announced the army intention to make Idi Amin-Dada Life President of Uganda.

On 27th June 1976, an Air France plane is hijacked by Palestinian guerrillas of PLO and brought to Entebbe Airport. Idi Amin-Dada pretended to handle the negotiations.

On July 4th 1976, Israeli Commandos raided Entebbe Airport to free the 100 hostages on an Air France place.

On July 4th, 1976, Britain broke off diplomatic relations with Uganda.

In October 1976, a Soviet Military delegate led by Gen. Vasilevskiy visited Kampala and agreed to replace military equipment including planes lost in the Israeli raid on Entebbe Airport.

This is how Idi Amin-Dada opted out of international diplomatic relations Uganda enjoyed with Britain our mentor to zero and scaling down to zero the cordial diplomatic relations Uganda once enjoyed with USA, a world super power which was almost tantamount to committing political suicide.

Another factor which played a major role in ousting Idi Amin-Dada out of power was the involvement of the Tanzania Peoples Defence Forces (TPDF) in the 1978-79 liberation war. Our desire to acquire military training was to enable us to come back to Uganda to even scores with Idi Amin-Dada. At the end of our military training, we thought that once in Uganda we shall embark on a classical armed struggle whereby we shall begin the war in rural areas, and we shall come to takeover power in the capital Uganda when we have gained massive strength that could off-set Idi Amin-Dada's forces.

However, once we had infiltrated into Uganda with all small arms, ammunitions and explosives at our disposal, I was a bit surprised when our leaders based outside Uganda ordered us to hit urban targets[169]. And, it never occurred to me that Tanzania was going to be involved directly with us in the struggle.

But as I have already mentioned before, once State Research Bureau personnel arrested three of our combatants, they tortured them and extracted a lot of information from them regarding what we were up to. Having known what we intended to do, Idi Amin-Dada told the world the truth that Tanzania, had invaded Uganda much as the world might not have believed in what he was saying. As I have already mentioned also, Idi Amin-Dada then decided not to wait for the massive invasion from Tanzania, he decided to take the war to Tanzania.

> On 9th October 1978, hence, as a result, Idi Amin-Dada's troops invaded Tanzania, on the 16th Anniversary of Uganda's Independence.

By doing this, Idi Amin-Dada made it possible for us to get a formidable ally that helped Uganda's credible fighting group to fight him out of power. When we were being trained in

---

[169] See THE D-Day and ITS EFFECT; Ibids 72 & 156 & 158

Tanzania, we did not get wind of Tanzania's future involvement in ousting Idi Amin-Dada out of power.

As far as we fighters of SUM were concerned, this was the more wonderful thing the Almighty God did to save his people in Uganda in 1979. Tanzania, in our estimation became a brother in need, a brother indeed! Without the direct involvement of Tanzania in the 1978-79 liberation war, no one would tell for certain how long the liberation war against Idi Amin-Dada could have lasted between Uganda fighting group and Idi Amin-Dada's troops. But, with the direct involvement of TPDF, alas, the rest was history.

The role SUM fighters played in the war was also one of the factors which helped in the liberation war of ousting Idi Amin-Dada out of power. When we hit the three targets in Kampala, the following day there was a rally at '...Mnazi Moja...' in Dar es Salaam. In his speech during the rally, Mwalimu Julius Nyerere gave us, SUM fighters, a glowing tribute. He told his fellow countrymen that Tanzania had courageous children who had managed to hit Idi Amin-Dada within Uganda in his capital city.

Previously, during the June 1971 Organisation of African Unity (OAU) Heads of State Summit in Addis Ababa, other African countries led by Nigeria accused Tanzania of naked aggression in invading Uganda.

This time Mwalimu Julius Nyerere defended Tanzanians by addressing that summit's accusation that there was war within Uganda itself. This war within Uganda was being waged by fighters of SUM.

If we had not re-started the 1978-79 war of liberation within Uganda, the realistic scenario of Tanzania's invasion of Uganda then could have been different. In retaliation to Idi Amin-Dada's invasion of Kagera Salient, Tanzania could have used her right of hot pursuit and fought off Idi Amin-Dada's troops perhaps up to Mbarara and Masaka, destroying these towns in revenge for what

Idi Amin-Dada's troops did in Kagera Salient, then they could have withdrawn back to Tanzania.

So without any exaggeration what-so-ever, the role we played in the 1978-79 liberation war was modest but crucial, since it made it possible for the Tanzania Peoples Defence Forces (TPDF) to invade Uganda and fight Idi Amin-Dada out of power. The role we played exonerated Tanzania in any violation of International law.

When Idi Amin-Dada assumed power in 1971, his frequent purges of officers who appeared enlightened was another factor which helped in the liberation of Uganda from his hands in 1979. The frequent purges of officers served to weed out experienced officers from Idi Amin-Dada's army; the result was a weak army of illiterate mercenaries who were always ready to kill and torture in order to generate fear in the population. In this army of illiterate, ill-trained, and inexperienced mercenaries, much as its personnel were heavily armed, they could not stand their ground at then military confrontation with the TPDF.

The TPDF was a modern army, which was being led by learned offices, operating support weapons which Idi Amin-Dada's army did not have. After a devastating bombing campaign against the towns of Masaka and Mbarara, the TPDF moved steadily and neutralised the heavily armed but ill-trained and demoralised troops of Idi Amin-Dada. As the Tanzania troops moved closer to Kampala, the population welcomed them warmly especially in Western Uganda.

Development in the military front was also one of the factors which helped a great deal in the liberation war of 1978-79.

> On 26th March 1979, on the basis of development on the military front, Ugandan politicians had to be forced into a compromise to form a united front in Moshi for the purpose of replacing a defeated dictatorship.

After days of squabbling, the **Uganda National Liberations Front** [UNLF] a product of over 20 Ugandan political and military groups was born. The UNLF summarised their programme as Unity, Democracy, and National Independence.

Another factor which contributed to the liberation of Uganda from the hands of Idi Amin-Dada in 1979 was the blood of Church of Uganda Archbishop Janani Luwum[170]. As already stated that, on the 16th February 1977, murder of the three prominent Ugandans, namely, Archbishop Janani Luwum, Wilson Erinayo Oryema[171] and Charles Oboth Ofumbi[172], marked the turning point in Idi Amin-Dada's regime to hold Uganda together.

The murders had awakened much of the world to the brutalities of the regime and a concerted campaign to remove Idi Amin-Dada took a new turn with church blessing as world leaders especially in the US, Britain, Canada and elsewhere were urged to double their efforts towards that end.

> The beginning of 1977 saw a further deterioration in state-church relations in Uganda as church leaders openly accused the regime of misuse of authority and discrimination in favour of Muslims.
>
> In early February 1977, Archbishop Janani Luwum's official residence at Namirembe was searched for arms but nothing like arms was found. In Tororo, Bishop Yona Okoth was threatened with arrest.
>
> On 5th February 1977, Radio Uganda announced the finding of arms near the Archbishops' residence by school children.

---

[170] Ibid 13
[171] Ibid 14
[172] Ibid 15

On 9th – 11th February 1977, the Anglican Bishops meeting took place in Kampala while their Catholic colleagues were also deliberating.

On 10th February 1977, there was a pastoral letter by Bishops of Church of Uganda protesting harassments of the church's leadership and Christians in general and accusing armed forces of atrocities.

Among the issues which the bishops listed as causing a lot of concern were insecurity, preferential treatment of Muslims, confiscation of private property, excessive power of the notorious intelligence organs – State Research Bureau (SRB) – agents and increased role of external (Arabs) forces in Uganda affairs.

Within a week, Idi Amin-Dada had not only castigated and abused the Archbishop, but arrested and murdered him in a faked car accident along with two government Ministers, Lt. Col. Erinayo Wilson Oryema[173] and Mr Charles Oboth-Ofumbi[174], all of whom he implicated in a planned coup d'état.

But the late Archbishop Janani Luwum's[175] blood was not shed in vain. It led to the whole world consensus of need for the removal of Idi Amin-Dada from power, effected two years in 1979 after the Archbishop was killed.

The Late Archbishop Janani Luwum was a humble servant of Almighty God. His entourage proffers they had not seen him lose his temper even once. Like a good shepherd who is always loved by his sheep, Archbishop Janani Luwum was very much loved by the Christians of the Northern Uganda Diocese he shepherded. His former entourage assert that his consecration was different from any other consecrations of any of the six Bishops that diocese have had. When Janani Luwum was being consecrated

---

[173] Ibid 14
[174] Ibid 15
[175] Ibid 13

Bishop of Northern Uganda, so many Christians turned up that day in 1969 that they did not fit in St Phillips' Cathedral in Gulu. The venue for his consecration was then switched to Pece Stadium.

On 18th January 2015 while giving a talk as '...*Great Achievers...*' over Radio Mega 102 FM, Gulu, Rev Canon Wilson Obura, who was one of the pupils of Janani Luwum in P4 in 1948 compared his death to that of Jesus Christ. He told his audience that there were similarities to what happened the day the late Archbishop was killed to what happened when Jesus Christ was crucified.

On 16th February 1977 when Idi Amin-Dada was addressing religious leaders, diplomats and members of Defence Council at the International Conference Centre (ICC) Kampala, Rev Canon Wilson Obura stated that Idi Amin-Dada alleged that some arms were found near the home of the late Archbishop. He then asked his audience what should be done with the Archbishops. Members of the Defence council and some of the soldiers who were part of the audience shouted in chorus that he should be killed. By doing this, they played the role of Jews who shouted that Jesus Christ should be impaled when Pontius Pilate asked them what he should do with Jesus Christ.

Rev Canon Wilson Obura told his audience that the day the late Archbishop Janani Luwum was killed there was a partial eclipse of the sun. We recall that when Jesus died on the stake at 03.00pm, there was darkness up to 06.00pm due to the eclipse of the sun.

Rev Canon Wilson Obura also stated that the blood of Archbishop Janani Luwum liberated Ugandan from their political sins much as the blood of Jesus Christ set us free from our sins so long as we have faith in him.

The Archbishop, like Jesus Christ was killed with two others. Jesus Christ was killed together with two other criminals as the Archbishop Janani Luwum was killed together with Ministers Lt

Col Erinayo Wilson Oryema[176] and Charles Oboth-Ofumbi[177] who were assumed criminals.

The **State Research Bureau**[178] (SRB) personnel who killed Archbishop Janani Luwum shared among themselves his clerical robes the way the Roman soldiers shared among themselves Jesus's garments. No one knows what clerical robe of the late Archbishop that Idi Amin-Dada took since it was stated that he was the one who killed the Archbishop by shooting him in the mouth.

The late Archbishop like Jesus Christ knew about his impending death. On 11th February 1977, according to Rev Canon Wilson Obura, when the Archbishop was giving his last Bible study to the House of Bishops, he cited what Jesus Christ told the Jews; John 8:21.

He told the House of Bishops that;

"...where I am going you cannot come..."

During the Bible Study the Archbishop also cited a text in the Bible where it is stated that when the good shepherd is struck, his sheep will run away. This was what happened when the Archbishop was killed. Prominent Anglican religious leaders including Bishop Festus Kivengyere[179] of Kabale Diocese, Bishop Benon Ogwal[180] of Gulu Diocese, and Bishop Yona Okoth[181] of Bukedi Diocese went into exile.

After three days when the Archbishop was killed, some Anglican clerics claimed they saw the Archbishop in the sky at the face of the sun walking with two other persons.

---

[176] Ibid 13
[177] Ibid 15
[178] Ibid 4
[179] Ibid 140; was recalled by the ancestors in 1988.
[180] Second exile to the USA post-1986 under the NRA-regime of Yoweri Kaguta Museveni
[181] Was recalled by the ancestor in 2001

No wonder, the late Archbishop Janani Luwum was canonised as a Saint by the Anglican Church during its synod which took place in 1988. And since then the world has been celebrating 16th February as St Janani Luwum Day.

> On 16th February 2015 in Uganda, we have just begun doing this and the President of Uganda has declared 16th February of each year as a Public Holiday in Uganda.

The death of Archbishop Janani Luwum made the world close its eyes when TPDF assisted by credible Ugandan fighting groups to invade Uganda and fight Idi Amin-Dada out of power.

Idi Amin-Dada's nature and notably his character was one of the factors that led also to his overthrow. By character, Idi Amin-Dada was a very brutal person, obstinate and over confident. When he attained power on 13th February 1971, both nationals and foreigners did not know that he was a brutal man, yet he was. It was his, extensive populist manoeuvres which went ahead in all parts of Uganda which acted as smoke screens to cover up his brutalities as soon as he attained power.

Yet Idi Amin-Dada moved with force to eliminate his suspected opponents in the army whether real or imaginary. This led to extensive massacres of soldiers of the Langi and Acholi nationalities, who during Obote's rule were alleged to have formed the backbone of soldiery in all military units in the country. The campaign was a brutal one, involving the herding of victims into rooms that were then blown up with explosives. This sort of extermination campaign drives any would-be-threat in the army helped to entrench Idi Amin-Dada in power with the support of his clique of trusted **Non-Commissioned Officers (NCO)**[182] largely with Nubian origin whom he promoted hurriedly through

---

[182] This infers to the military rank and file soldiers - who do not or have not attained a position of authority and/or is without practical knowledge and experience of exercising authority.

the ranks. Promotions do not buy or give experience or more military skills. Experience implies practical learning to gain skills. Hence, without the requisite skills and experience, Idi Amin-Dada troops could not stand at the military front faced with a well-trained, disciplined and experienced **Tanzania Peoples Defence Forces (TPDF)** with their Uganda allies during liberation.

As his list of victims grew, so did his insecurity and number of opponents. At the beginning of his rule, his opponents were soldiers of Lango and Acholi nationalities. But as times moved on Idi Amin-Dada went on eliminating even his fellow soldiers of Kakwa nationality from the army during his rule. Brig Charles Arube[183] was a point in case. He even attempted to kill his Vice President Mustafa Adrisi[184], a fellow Kakwa in a planned motor accident. He even murdered Lt Col Ondoga[185], all from the same West Nile[186] area. By doing all this Idi Amin-Dada unknowingly was mobilising the entire country against his rule. Perhaps this explains the demoralisation of his troops by the time the liberation war came in 1978-79 against him.

Brutalities serve only to divide people. Healing wounds caused by brutalities is not easy since we Africans by nature believe in revenge or reparation whenever one's relatives have been brutally murdered. Whenever a brutal leader leaves power there will be horizontal violence against the favourite nationalities that had perpetuated the slaughter of members of other nationalities whom were assumed to be their political arch-enemies. This was what happened when Idi Amin-Dada was ousted from power in Uganda in 1979.

By nature, Idi Amin-Dada seemed to be somebody who was obstinate. In a weighty matter of attacking another country he could have brought this matter in the governing cabinet. If he

---

[183] Ibid 143
[184] Recalled by the ancestors in 2013
[185] Ibid 143
[186] Ibid 143

did, he might have been given the pros and cos of the matter. But over confident and obstinate as he was, he went ahead regardless of the advice he was given against invading Tanzania. His failure to heed advice led him to make a precious mistake which enabled him to lose power to the benefit of oppressed Ugandans.

Was overconfidence to do with his body size, his being a former heavy-weight boxing champion of Uganda or his folly?? It seemed the word impossible did not belong in the Idi Amin-Dada dictionary. He went to the extent of challenging Mwalimu Julius Nyerere for a boxing match. We, the fighters of SUM brought Mwalimu Nyerere's acceptance of that boxing match with Idi Amin-Dada by hitting three targets in Kampala. And the result of that boxing match is now history. Mwalimu Julius Nyerere, out-foxed, out-boxed, and knocked out Idi Amin-Dada in the boxing contest.

When the war became too hot for Idi Amin-Dada, he appealed for support from Buganda. He warned them that if they failed to support him, their arch-enemy, Dr Apollo Milton Obote would come back to rule Uganda once more. He urged his largely illiterate ill-trained soldiers to fight hard and face Tanzania Peoples Defence Force (TPDF) with all the courage required. He told his soldiers that he allowed them to bring their chickens and goats to their homes in urban areas. Idi Amin-Dada appealed even to the Pope at the Vatican to tell Julius Nyerere to stop fighting. But his fate was what over-confidence brings. The Holy Father did nothing. Praise be to him.

In a nutshell, factors which led to the ouster of Idi Amin-Dada from power were:
- The collapse of the economy that intensified local negative sentiments to his regime, his living to the extreme by his famous adage of;

> *"...there is no permanent friendship and enmity in politics...",*

this led him to forsake cordial diplomatic relations which he enjoyed with the West at the beginning of his rule leading to international diplomatic isolation.

- As the list of his victims grew, so did his insecurity and numbers of his opponents. Hence, in fear of his development, he wanted to arm his army up to the teeth such that he would withstand any attack that would come against his regime.
- The need of arming his army up to the teeth could not be met by his western allies, so he was compelled to forsake the cordial diplomatic relations with them. He opted for cordial diplomatic relations with Arab countries who were ready to give *"...every assistance to Uganda Army...",* particularly through Libya. As a result, Idi Amin-Dada ended up serving Arab cause until he was ousted out of power.
- The invasion of Tanzania was a costly mistake which Idi Amin-Dada made and when Tanzania in turn invaded Uganda assisted by Ugandan fighting groups spearheaded by SUM made it possible for Idi Amin-Dada to be ousted out of power in 1979.
- The frequent purges of officers who appeared enlightened rendered his army devoid of well-trained, experienced military personnel. In the end, his army had predominantly illiterate, ill-trained, and inexperienced military personnel that was no match to the modern, well-trained, well-equipped, and experienced TPDF.
- The development at the military front was very encouraging; forcing Ugandan politicians in the diaspora into a compromise to form a united front for the purpose of replacing a defeated dictatorship.

- The blood of Church of Uganda Archbishop Janani Luwum was nit shed in vain. His murder with two other important Ugandan marked the turning point in Idi Amin-Dada's regime holding Uganda together. It awakened much of the world to the brutalities of the regime and a concerted campaign to remove Idi Amin-Dada from power took a new turn with the church's blessing.
- Idi Amin-Dada's nature and his character; pompous, arrogant, brutal, obstinate and over-confidence led to his ouster from power. And his lack of education might have played a role in his removal from power too. He joined Kings African Rifles (KAR)[187] from a lower primary level. He leant to speak English when he was already President of Uganda. Due to his level of education; it could be assumed that he was not able to think critically though valuable advice he was being given by his well-wishers in all his endeavours leading to costly mistake.

Afterword 2:

THE AFTERMATH

I recall what my history teacher, Mr Kahangi told us about unity in Uganda in 1970 when he was teaching us about the role nationalism played to enable Uganda to achieve her independence in 1962 from the British. I was then in Senior 4 preparing to sit for my 'O' Level Examination ('O' Level is equivalent to GSCE – General School Certificate of Education). He told us that we Ugandans were capable of forging unity whenever there was a major problem facing us, we could unite

---

[187] Ibid 70

and get rid of that problem. Once we have solved that problem, we would fall back to our original positions.

I saw this at play in 1979 and thereafter when several military and political groups were forced by circumstances to unite for the purposes of getting rid of Idi Amin-Dada from power. Once they got rid of Idi Amin-Dada on 11th April 1979, thereafter, the various groups fell back to their original positions.

Another thing is that in politics when you have several political and military groups fighting together to solve a given problem, once they have solved it, they will embark on fighting another to gain or regain political power. This too is what happened in 1979, after the ouster of Idi Amin-Dada from power.

Save Uganda Movement [SUM], much as it had faith in the principles of Uganda National Liberation Front [UNLF], was fought ruthlessly by Kikosi Maalum (KM) of Dr Obote's, and Front for National Salvation [FRONASA] of Yoweri Museveni. The two forces did everything possible within their power to exclude fighters of SUM from being integrated into the officer's corps of Uganda National Liberation Army [UNLA], at the beginning of the integration process of integrating all the various fighting groups into UNLA.

Once we had got rid of Idi Amin-Dada, FRONASA played its cards close to its chest by not expressing dislike for SUM fighters. But KM commanders did not hide any dislike from SUM. Lt. Col. David Oyite Ojok, in particular, used to complain openly that Tanzania over trained us. He also wanted to know what they, as Dr Milton Obote's group, were not informed of the presence of SUM in Tanzania.

He even stated several times that fighters of SUM were a dangerous lot that should not be near anybody.

Lt. Col. David Oyite Ojok and then Inspector General of Uganda Police Force (IGP), David Barlow went to the extent of making preparation at Makindye Military Barracks so that we would be arrested and detained there.

We were only saved from this fate by the intervention of Capt. Simbei and other senior Tanzania Peoples Defence Forces (TPDF) officers. They told Lt. Col. David Oyite Ojok to prepare a statement for the President of Tanzania which they will take to Nyerere once we have been arrested and detained. They told him that if he did not like us Tanzania was ready to give us Tanzania citizenship, employ us, give us land, and marry for us. With this kind of remark from high ranking TPDF officers, Lt. Col. David Oyite Ojok cowed down!

But the intervention of high-ranking TPDF officers did not deter Lt. Col. David Oyite Ojok from making sure that we the fighters of SUM who were infiltrated into Uganda from Tanzania to start the liberation war against Idi Amin-Dada from within Uganda were not integrated into the officer corps of UNLA. This was done at the beginning of the integration process of the various fighting groups into UNLA.

Yet after the liberation war, we reliably learnt that the TPDF sent their appraisal and recommendation about every one of the 40 members of the Special Forces that was infiltrated into Uganda to start the war. However, these appraisals and recommendations of the TPDF were ignored by the leadership/command of UNLA.

Mr Yoweri Museveni was the then Minister of Defence in the UNLF government. He is known to be a vocal person who speaks up when something is getting out of hand. I wish to state that he did not utter anything about us. What did his silence mean? We took this silence to mean consent.

I have never heard both Mr Yoweri Museveni and Lt. Col. David Oyite Ojok expressing appreciation about the role SUM played during the war of liberating Uganda against Idi Amin-Dada. Now and then senior military officers from the Dr Obote's forces used to come up with unfriendly remarks that SUM did not do anything during the war of liberation against Idi Amin-Dada worth mentioning. Against these doubts, one asks two questions:

a. Who were those who liberated Kitgum[188] before even the arrival there of the liberators from Tanzania? And;
b. Which fighting group started the war against Idi Amin-Dada from within Uganda then?[189]

There also were only two answers:

ai. SUM fighters started the liberation war against Idi Amin-Dada from within Uganda after which other fighting forces joined them.

bi. It was SUM fighters that made it possible for Tanzania and other Ugandan fighting groups to invade Uganda[190] and fight Idi Amin-Dada out of power in accordance with International Law.

In our view, other Ugandan fighting groups were not men enough since they failed to start the war of liberation against Idi Amin-Dada from within Uganda. They were just escorted home by TPDF. The major task they performed was covering long distances on foot from Tanzania to Uganda.

It is not by coincidence therefore that one would find no mention of SUM in any literature written by **Front for National Salvation (FRONASA)** of Mr Yoweri Museveni, and **Uganda Peoples Congress (UPC)** of Dr Apollo Milton Obote. This fact is by design. Many individuals have been given medals for fighting against Idi Amin-Dada. But many of us who started the war that led to the overthrow of Idi Amin-Dada's regime have never been mentioned nor accorded such medals - Why? Because Mr Yoweri Museveni in particular and by subterfuge, **National Resistance Movement [NRM]** want to take all the credit from the 1978-79 liberation

---

[188] Ibid 57 & 68
[189] This question is posed this way because of the SUM Modus Operandi of '...*Need to know*...' There were triggers/actions by other SUM cells that I was not privy to and/or was never or have been shared with me. I have no doubt it my minds that each anti-Amin action was well coordinated
[190] See Ibid 156 which informs this summation.

war! much as I would not wish to be awarded a medal[191] for war against my own countrymen.

Idi Amin-Dada stayed in power for about 8 years because in the opposition to get rid of him were some individuals who believed that they had personal office to regain. If anybody in opposition who did not agree with them tried to champion a course of overthrowing Idi Amin-Dada's regime, and they got wind of it they would reveal the matter to Idi Amin-Dada. This leaking of information to Idi Amin-Dada normally was aimed at sabotaging efforts of those who were serious about removing Idi Amin-Dada from power. However, if such of removing Idi Amin-Dada was coming with the blessing of those who wanted to regain personal offices such efforts would not be leaked out to Idi Amin-Dada. Hence, each political or military group ranged against Idi Amin-Dada had to guard its secrets tightly from rival groups[192]. So, the struggle to remove Idi Amin-Dada from power was made difficult because of this kind of weakness among Ugandan ideal fighting groups.

A point in case is that of SUM. When Obote's men heard of the progress SUM was making against Idi Amin-Dada within Uganda they attempted to sabotage that effort. We suspected that Dr Milton Obote's group got this information from *'one'* of our combatants who remained in Kenya when we were being infiltrated into Uganda. We failed to know why *'he'* chose not to come into Uganda. What we know for sure was that *'he'* informed Dr Obote's men about the successes we were scoring against Idi Amin-Dada in the fighting inside Uganda. We suspect that person was Mr Tom Otuku, one of our own, who chose to be a traitor. In this regard;

---

[191] This is inferred from the NRA-War Medals being awarded by those who fought their Anti-Obote II government between 1981-1985. The intent of this act alone is to debase the Anti-Amin 1978-1979 liberation that triggered changes from Military Governance to democratic rule.

[192] Ibid 156

Save Uganda Movement [SUM]

the 2nd March 1979 attack on Tororo Air&Seaborne Garrison by Obote's men based in Kenya was uncalled for[193].

What was the aim of that attack? To alert Idi Amin-Dada about the dangers against him coming from Eastern Uganda then? This is why Dr Milton Obote's men carried out this attack alone without the participation of any fighting groups.

After the overthrow of Idi Amin-Dada and the entire Uganda was liberated, the time came for integration of all fighting groups into the rank and file of UNLA. We SUM fighters complied with that order by reporting to Mubende Military Barracks[194]. I led nearly all members of the Special Force of SUM who were infiltrated into Uganda to start the liberation war.

When all the fighting groups assembled at Mubende, there was a visit made by nearly all members of the Military Commission of UNLF. By this time, the UNLF leadership had exchanged hands three times. It was now, Military Commission, which was in charge of Uganda. During the visit, the UNLA Chief Of Staff, Lt. Col. David Oyite Ojok came with our own Commanders Col. Zedekiah Maruru and Col. William Omaria Lo'Arapai in tow. A meeting was held by these members of the **Military Commission**[195] with commanders of the various fighting groups. I attended that meeting as one of the commanders of SUM. I recall one remark which was made by the Chief of Staff, Lt. Col. David Oyite Ojok during the meeting which I found to be out of place. He told the meeting that other fighting groups should stop saying that SUM did not do anything during the war that ousted Idi Amin-Dada from power in 1979. I did not understand why he came up with this remark during the meeting. What was it supposed to achieve? He knew best!

---

[193] Ibid 88
[194] Ibid 156
[195] Ibid 42

After the meeting, members of the Military Commission went back to Kampala. Our Commanders: Col. Zedekiah Maruru and Col. William Omaria lo'Arapai did not spare any time to address us wherever we were in Mubende Military barracks. After this visit, we saw some soldiers from various fighting groups being selected to go for officers' course at Jinja Military barracks. Me, as one of the commanders of a fighting group was not informed to select some of my men to go for this course or elsewhere. Hence, none of us was considered for the officers' course.

After documentation and registration into the Uganda National Liberation Army (UNLA), I was given a number and told to report to Masindi Barracks where recruits or Non-Commissioned Officer[196] [NCO] was to be trained. All my men received the same order. We were not amused at all with this sort of discrimination. Here was a situation where illiterate and semi-illiterate soldiers were being sent for officers' course at the expense of educated soldiers. Were we going back to Idi Amin-Dada's era or we were moving forward? This was a real slap on our faces despite all we did for the liberation of our country from the hands of the tyrant! I refused to go to Masindi Barracks. I found it improper for me to go for training at Masindi Barracks. I got a pass and went to Kampala. I was wondering why our commanders did not see to it that some of us were integrated into officer corps of the UNLA? This had nothing to do with ambition on our part; it had to do with natural justice. With what we did, we deserved pursuing military career for the benefit of our country. But all our efforts towards this end were now being frustrated by those who thought they were well placed to regain or gain personal offices in Uganda. They were looking at us as stumbling blocks to their endeavours.

I kept wondering why our commanders did not see to it that some of us were integrated into the officer corps of UNLA. Were they also not appreciating what we did? Why have they left us to

---

[196] Ibid 156

fend for ourselves in the integration process? One of the realistic scenarios I could think of which made our commanders to leave us in the cold was the death of Lt. Col. John Ruhinda.

> On 31st July 1979 Lt. Col. John Ruhinda was murdered by UNLA and Tanzanian soldiers when he went to Makerere University to eat millet bread with some friends and relatives there.

Lt. Col. John Ruhinda apparently stood in the way of those who wanted to gain or regain personal offices in Uganda after the fall of Idi Amin-Dada. That was why he was killed in cold blood so that his death should serve as a serious warning to any senior military officer who dared to stand in the way of those who want to gain or regain personal offices in Uganda. Hence, our two commanders were scared out if their wits. The integration of fighters from various fighting groups had a lot to be desired. I have seen fighters from Kikosi Maalum (KM) who were commissioned after two weeks of military training and promoted up to the rank of Captain or Major. They might have been university graduates all right but giving them such ranks without going through officer cadets training course was uncalled for. Major Olwol and Captain Bob Odong Nayenda were points in case.

Another scenario I would think of which made our commanders to abandon us was the emergence of SUM itself. SUM was formed after a merger of two fighting groups; one formed by Mr Ateker Ejalu and another one formed by Engineer Akena p'Ojok and his colleagues. Mr Ateker Ejalu was the first to seek the assistance of Tanzania government. Engineer Akena p'Ojok[197] later went for the same with his colleagues to the Tanzania government. Tanzania government advised Engineer Akena p'Ojok to join force with Ateker Ejalu[198] to make it easy for Tanzania to help both fighting groups. Engineer Akena p'Ojok

---

[197] See Foreword; Flagpost 4
[198] Ibid 46

saw sense in this advice and complied, then **Save Uganda Movement (SUM)** came into being.

Ateker Ejalu expected to be the leader of SUM but other members of SUM made Akena p'Ojok de'facto leader of SUM[199]. The late Dennis Echwou told me that Ateker Ejalu was not happy with this state of affair. He swore that he was going to destroy SUM unless he was given its leadership, so what happened to SUM during their integration into the **Uganda National Liberation Army (UNLA)** ranks might have been the efforts of Mr Ateker Ejalu to destroy SUM. He might have advised our two commanders not to bother about seeing to it that we were integrated into UNLA. Our two commanders were not bothered about seeing to it that some of us fit into the rank of officer corps of UNLA. If Ateker Ejalu maliced us in his desire to destroy SUM because he was not given the leadership of SUM so be it. We accept his malice with honour knowing that we did our best to see to it that our country regained her dignity once more.

Going back, when I came to Kampala from Mubende I met **Benson Ogwang**[200], who then was heading **National Security Agency [NASA]**[201]. I explained to him our plight. He told me that there was opportunity for training in overt and covert security personnel in Cuba and Algeria. I opted for over security training in Algeria.

> On 10th March 1980 I went to Algeria for a 3-month overt security training when Mr Godfrey Lukongwa-Binaisa was President of Uganda.

Mr Godfrey Lukongwa-Binaisa met us at State House Entebbe since we were destined to be his VIP Security Personnel upon completion of our course. He addressed us, urged us to be patriotic, and bade us farewell.

---

[199] Ibid 198
[200] Previous roles were Head of Presidential Security 1966-1971 and 1979-1980.
[201] State security agency formed post-1980 in the Obote II government.

When we reached Algeria, our instructors were not happy with the duration of 3 months. They told us that their government had requested Uganda government to send us for at least one year. They wondered how they were going to cover all the course content for VIP Protection just for 3 months.

Nevertheless, we embarked on the VIP Protection course, as a crash programme. As part of our training, we did Martial Art and Karate, but since the course was short, we advanced up to Yellow Belt. They advised us strongly to continue with the Karate training in Uganda up to the Black Belt level.

In weapons training, we practiced shooting with all weapons Very Important Person (VIP) Security personnel needs to perform their duties. We practiced shooting at the shooting range with revolver, Makarov Pistols, SMG, Telescopic guns, etc. The subject matter of our course entailed the meaning of Very Important Person (VIP) Protection and what it takes to carry out VIP protection at the residence, in a convoy, in the office, and at the venue where the VIP is supposed to be. We finished this 3-month overt security course and came back to Uganda in May 1980 knowing that our going to Algeria was a wasted effort because those who mattered in Uganda then sabotaged it.

> On 12th May 1980, a six-member Military Commission (MC) under chairmanship of Mr Paulo Muwanga[202] and Mr Yoweri Museveni as Vice Chairman had taken over the state and Mr Godfrey Lukongwa-Binaisa was put under house arrest at State House, Entebbe.

We came back to Uganda when Mr Godfrey Lukongwa-Binaisa[203] was no longer President of Uganda given frequent changes in leadership during the Uganda National Liberation Front (UNLF) era. Since the perception was that we were supposed to be VIP Protection security personnel for him we were not deployed.

---

[202] Also had served as a Uganda's Ambassador to France.
[203] Ibid 89.

However, some of us found our way of serving as security personnel of some Ministers.

Those of us who were not deployed elsewhere decided to gather intelligence information for our leaders. We were operating from the Suite of Hon Minister Akena p'Ojok at Nile Mansion Hotel, opposite the suite of UNLA Chief of Staff Lt. Col. David Oyite Ojok. We used to feed the Chief of Staff with any sensitive information we deemed to be of national importance even though he was also operating a small intelligence unit in his suite.

Towards General Elections of 10th - 11th December 1980, our reliable informer in Kenya Police Special Branch informed us that the Democratic Party (DP) was importing fake ballot papers for purposes of rigging the General Elections. The fake ballot papers, Kenya Police Special Branch had discovered in two brand new pick-ups which the DP had imported for their political campaign. We informed Hon Minister Akena p'Ojok about this and he directed us to inform Chief of Staff immediately about this. We did this.

After getting this information, we later learnt about the comment the Chief of Staff made that we were a dangerous group that should not be near anybody. I even informed Hon Minister Prof. Ephraim Kamuntu about the importation of fake ballot papers by the DP. Let me hope that he still remembers this!

Having informed the Chief of Staff about this, we requested our informer to inform their counterpart in Uganda about the import. Our informer accordingly informed Uganda Police Special Branch about this. When these two pick-ups entered Uganda with their fake ballot papers, they were impounded by Uganda Police. The Officer in Charge (OC) Malaba Police Station informed us of this development and demanded that we should go and collect the two pick-ups from Malaba with their fake papers.

We once again informed Chief of Staff about this development. We had high hopes that he would avail us with transport and some soldiers so that we could go to Malaba to bring these pick-ups to Kampala with their fake ballot papers. To our great disappointment the Uganda National Liberation Army (UNLA) Chief of Staff Lt. Col. David Oyite Ojok did nothing. Up to now I do not know why he did this. Later on, we reliably learnt that these two pick-ups were released from Malaba with their fake ballot papers intact and found their way to the DP Headquarters in Kampala. The Officer in Charge (OC) of Malaba Police Station was compelled to release the two pick-ups due to the fact that we failed to go to collect them.

I seriously took note of the fact that the UNLA Chief of Staff Lt. Col. David Oyite Ojok was one of these Ugandan leaders who shy away from critical decisions when faced with a given reality. This was the same thing, according to Apollo Ejou[204], that Dr Milton Obote did when he had all the information with credible evidence that Idi Amin-Dada was going to overthrow his government. Dr Obote could have ordered for the arrest of Idi Amin-Dada immediately before proceeding for the Commonwealth Heads of State Summit in Singapore, but he did not do so. If anything, he delegated the whole matter to his trusted senior security officers. The kind of suffering Ugandans went through under Idi Amin-Dada's regime could have been avoided if a prompt critical decision was taken by Dr Milton Obote to stop him. I could see the repeat of this kind of weakness in taking prompt decision in the UNLA Chief of Staff, Lt. Col. David Oyite Ojok. Well, as the English saying goes;

'...history repeating itself...'

Our sincere hope was that such omission would not amount to anything bad!

---

[204] Ibid 29

The frequent changes of leadership of Uganda during the Uganda National Liberation Front (UNLF) era meant that the UNLF had already outlived its usefulness. It implied no efforts by leaders of credible fighting groups to regain or gain state power in Uganda. We understood this fact quite so well that we embarked on preparing SUM for the eventuality of capturing state power through democratic means in view of the impending General Election of 10th - 11th December 1980.

The challenge at hand was to transform Save Uganda Movement (SUM) into a political party. To begin with we formed a Manifesto Committee composed of Mr Jacob Okello-Agwa, Eng. Jack Oita Alecho[205], Mr Sam Kisense[206], Mr Silver Gidongo[207], Mr Albert Lukwiya, Eng. Leo Obonyo and me to come up with a political Manifesto for SUM. We agreed to meet in the office of Mr Jacob Okello Agwa[208], Principal Economist, Ministry of Planning and Economic Development at Uganda House, Kampala. We used to meet in the lunch hours to write the manifesto and sooner or later it was ready. The next step was for our leaders to look for funding from progressive countries to finance the party. Their efforts to this end did not bear fruit because they were late. During the UNLF era Dr Apollo Milton Obote was quiet in Tanzania but was not sleeping, he kept on sending the Uganda Peoples Congress (UPC) emissaries to look for funds from progressive countries of the world he could think of. When our leaders reached there and requested for funding of our political party, we were advised to join forces with the UPC. The Front for National Salvation (FRONASA) made efforts to join forces with

---

[205] Continued working with Uganda Airlines as Flight Engineer up to 1987. At the same time between 1980-1985 served as adviser to Maj. Gen. David Oyite Ojok, then Army Chief of Staff and also Vice President Paulo Muwanga; Board Director for Produce Marketing Board 1980-1987; and that of Uganda National Cultural Centre 1986-1987.

[206] Served as Personal Assistant to Minister of Information, Dr Obyara David Anyoti 1981-1985; and later years as RDC under the NRA-regime.

[207] See Notes 13

[208] Ibid 98

SUM to form Uganda Patriotic Movement [UPM] but this did not work out. SUM as a result was compelled to go back to UPC and it was SUM political manifesto which the UPC Manifesto Committee adopted as its working papers to come up with the 1980 UPC Manifesto.

The General Election of 10th - 11th December 1980 took place as scheduled. Immediately thereafter even when the Electoral Commission had started declaring results, members of the Democratic Party (DP) started celebrating that they had won the 1980 General Election. Al Hajj Akbar Akaki Adoko Nekyon, one cousin brother to Dr Apollo Milton Obote, was the one spearheading this celebration. I was not amused at all by the behaviour of the DP members knowing very well that they had rigged the General Election by using fake ballots papers they imported in Uganda before the General Election.

When the Secretary of the Electoral Commission, Mr Vincent Ssekono, began declaring some of the results that the DP was in the lead. That was when the Chief of Staff of the UNLA, Lt. Col. David Oyite Ojok remembered very well what we were telling him before the General Election. At this juncture, he might have informed the Chairman of the Military Commission (MC), Paulo Muwanga to this effect. Mr Paulo Muwanga then ordered the Secretary of the Electoral Commission, Mr Vincent Ssekono to stop announcing the results of the General Election, that he will do this himself. No one knows what the 'MC' Chairman, Mr Paulo Muwanga did but the fact remains that the Uganda People Congress (UPC) won the 1980 General Election. And the defeated political parties cried foul-play immediately, despite knowing different.

Well, that was expected since the 'DP' was sure of winning because its members rigged the General Election by use of fake ballot papers they acquired through other means. The cry of foul-play continues to be asserted and over-stated by other political interests and parties. This was the reason Mr Yoweri

Museveni gave for starting his guerrilla attack in the Luwero Triangle[209].

> On 6th February 1981, he commanded a group of 26 men in the first guerrilla attack at Kabamba Military Training School, under the banner of Popular Resistance Army [PRA].
>
> On 27th February 1981 PRA declared its 'Bush War'. In June PRA merged with UFF to form NRA/M.
>
> On 14th April 1981 Dr Obote described guerrillas as 'bandits' from loser section of parties who lost deposits in elections.
>
> On 20th August 1981, Dr Obote opened National Council of UPC and declared war on '...bandits...'
>
> On 24th January 1982, Cardinal Emmanuel Kiwanuka Nsubuga met Dr Apollo Milton Obote and proposed '...peace talk...' with so-called '...bandits...'

But Dr Milton Obote declined this offer because no '...peace talk...' to that effect took place. The '...Bush War...' continued in Luwero Triangle leading to loss of lives and property wherever it went until:

> On 25th-26th January 1986 when the National Resistance Army/Movement (NRA/M) took power.

But matters could have been helped if the information about importation of fake ballot papers were handled well by the UNLA Chief of Staff Lt. Col. David Oyite Ojok. If Lt. Col. David Oyite Ojok had availed us with transportation and soldiers we could have gone to Malaba and collected the two pick-ups containing the fake ballot papers. Those who had imported fake ballot papers could have been known and no one in his rightful mind

---

[209] This was a District to the north of Kampala City. I've not found or was privy to an explanation on how the description '...triangle...' came be applied.

could have gone about alleging foul-play after the General Election. It was the negligence of the UNLA Chief of Staff Lt. Col. David Oyite Ojok which led to some people to come up with the allegation of foul-play after the General Election of 1980.

Because of lack of ability by the UNLA Chief of Staff, Lt. Col. David Oyite Ojok to handle security matters right, Uganda was plunged into a 5-year '...Bush War...' which led even to his own death;

> On 12th December 1983, with other senior UNLA officers in a helicopter accident in Luwero while he was inspecting the war zone.

His hatred for SUM or greed for power had taken him nowhere.

When the NRA/M assumed power under the leadership of Yoweri Museveni, a civil war between Lord's Resistance Army (LRA[210]), and Uganda Peoples Defence Forces (UPDF)[211] went on for almost 20 years in '...Acholiland...' leading to a considerable loss of lives, property and lost development opportunity there. The Luwero '...Bush War...' and the civil war in Northern Uganda could have been avoided if then Chief of Staff Lt. Col. David Oyite Ojok had properly handled the information we gave him about importation of fake ballot papers. But he did nothing to the detriment of victims of these two senseless wars in Luwero 1980-1985; and consequently in '...Acholiland...' from 1986 on under the NRA-regime

I wish to re-state that I was mentally prepared to go through the problems which faced us after participating in the war that ousted Idi Amin-Dada. I was mentally prepared because during our military training in Tanzania in 1977-78, Captain Kaluzi, who led the training team, warned us about the fate which awaited us. Captain Kaluzi had a wealth of experience in Training African

---

[210] This is supposed to have come to an end after the Juba Peace Process concluded in 2008, however to date some below the radar fighting goes on.
[211] As in Ibid 214 supported by the US Forces

guerrilla fighters. He trained Mozambiquans, Angolans, Zimbabweans, and Namibians among other African guerrilla fighters. He saw how some of the fighters he trained fared after liberating their countries. He told us, one day during the course of our training that in the struggle we have embarked in, once we have succeeded either we shall be rewarded or rejected with empty hands, that is without any rewards whatsoever. At worse, some of us would escape with our own dear lives by the grace of God.

Therefore, what happened to us did not take me especially by surprise whatsoever. After all, one of the eternal tragedies of politics is that great ends can afterwards be achieved only by means which rob the ends of much of their worth. We did our best to save our country from the tyrannical rule of Idi Amin-Dada. At the end, what happened to us should be expected from any mechanic of any revolution.

Afterword 3:

RUMINATION

After Idi Amin-Dada has been ousted from power I met a friend, Mr Sam Bwolya, who asked me about what I did during the war of liberation. I told him what I did. However, my dear friend was not amused with what I told him. He then narrated to me a story about a cow, a hen, and pig;

> "...Each of them took turns to promise their masters what they were going to do to demonstrate their love for him..."
>
> "...The cow told her master she loved him so much and she will demonstrate that love by giving her master milk when the situation permits..."
>
> "...The hen told her master that she will do this by giving her master eggs when the situation permits..."
>
> "...Then finally, the pig on the other hand told his master that he will demonstrate this by giving him pork when the situation permits..."

I well understood the sense of his story. My friend was trying to tell me that I behaved like a pig in the sense that a pig normally has to sacrifice his very life to give pork to his master. My dear friend was telling me that I nearly sacrificed my life to save Uganda from the hands of Idi Amin-Dada. In so doing I behaved as a pig.

But far from it, I am not a pig but a human being who has the ability to think rationally about any course of action I am going to take and its consequences. I was a person who was politically conscious, and it was this that drove me to do what I did. To liberate Uganda from the hands of Idi Amin-Dada called for self-sacrificing Ugandans to volunteer for this cause. If by doing so as an individual is behaving like a pig, so be it.

In any case, since time immemorial, this is how well-meaning personalities have been looking at guerrillas fighters. Mazzini said of the great Italian guerrilla chief Garibaldi that:

> "...he had a Heart of Gold and the Brain of an Ox..."

English poet Tennyson spoke of Garibaldi as:

> "...possessing divine stupidity of a hero..."

May be such descriptions also befits me.

One day after the ouster of Idi Amin-Dada from power, I also met my dear brother who was my dear friend, Mr John Bitariho, when he learnt that I participated in the liberation war against Amin. He asked me a tough question which I think I might have failed to answer to the satisfaction of his inquiring mind. He asked me;

> "...well, Mr Opobo I have seen many of those who took part in the liberation war against Idi Amin-Dada materially doing very well, what have you done for yourself in this respect?

I told him that;

> "...mine was a self-sacrificing act of a volunteer in which no material gain was expected with immediate effect...
>
> "...I volunteered to do this without expecting any material gain whatsoever for my action...

I went on to tell him;

> "...that personally, I did not do anything for myself because our political leaders too did nothing to that effect; they did not reward us materially...
>
> "...They expected us to pursue military career and to be rewarded in the national army by way of promotion...
>
> "...It is so unfortunate that things did not work out as they as well as we expected...

I went on to inform my dear friend that;

> "...during the UNLF era I have been lobbying to honourable members of National Consultative Council [NCC] that Ugandans who aspire to join our Army must have a basic

> qualification equivalent to General School Certificate of Education [GSCE]...
>
> "...I am grateful to the fact that this policy has succeeded beyond our expectation in Uganda, since UNLA era in 1979...
>
> "...Much as I have already stated that I was mentally prepared for whatever fate I met after the liberation war of 1979, it does not mean that I was not hurt...
>
> "...I am a human being with feelings like any human being. I was of course hurt for being denied the opportunity to pursue a military training career after the liberation war..."

Now and then, I used to be consoled by the late Mr Jacob Okello-Agwa[212] who was one of the political leaders of Save Uganda Movement. He was in exile in Kenya in Kenya since 1971 when Idi Amin-Dada came to power. He spent all his time, money, and energy in the liberation of Uganda from the hands of Idi Amin-Dada. To me Jacob became a dear friend and a brother. He used to console me a great deal whenever I expressed bitterness for our fate. May his soul rest in eternal peace!

SUM did what any patriotic Ugandans would have done for the love of their country. The questions my two friends asked me kept on coming back in my mind. I knew that much as I have tried to answer them, I was not perhaps candid enough in doing so. I was compelled to ask myself several questions and answer them candidly to reach the bottom of the matter. What tangible benefits has my participation in the liberation of Uganda from the hands of Idi Amin-Dada brought to Ugandans? Will our struggle against Idi Amin-Dada end violation of human rights and excessive oppression of our people by our would-be leaders? And, was our success in ousting Idi Amin-Dada from power going to bring lasting peace and security that will enable Ugandans to live harmoniously forever!

---

[212] Ibid 5, 106

The answers to all these questions were NO! I was then forced to pose more questions to myself. If the answers to all the previous questions were NO! NO! NO! then what have we done for our country? What realities have we accepted in respect to Uganda politics? And, what facts that if we must live permanently in peace, security, stop blood-spilling, and destruction of property and wastage of valuable time for economic development in Uganda have we recognised?

To begin with, our struggle against Idi Amin-Dada was not a panacea to all political evils Uganda is destined to face. Our struggle therefore will not end violation of human rights by would be leaders of Uganda that will proceed Idi Amin-Dada and stop wastage of valuable time for economic development of Uganda. It is up to Ugandans to desist from encouraging tyrannical leaders like Idi Amin-Dada to come into power and rule them in Uganda. Our struggle to oust Idi Amin-Dada from power was just a step in the right direction. It was an opportunity to enable Ugandans to begin anew but more intelligently to put out in place a new arrangement in our Constitution by which we shall live in peace and security and harmoniously forever. Having ousted Idi Amin-Dada from power we have given an opportunity to Ugandans to come to a round table and willingly agree to make a new arrangement in our Constitution by which we shall live in peace and security for ever.

We have also accepted two realities and recognised the fact that we must permanently stop blood-spilling and destruction of property among ourselves and to stop wasting of valuable time for development we must go back to the drawing table willingly to make a new arrangement in our Constitution by which we shall live harmoniously for ever.

Secondly, we must also, accept another reality that there are different peoples in Uganda; the strength of our national unity will be in "...*Unity in Diversity*..." We must therefore realise and accept a system in our Constitution that will enable us to enjoy the highest degree of stability and as consequence prosperity.

It therefore goes without say that the original arrangement under which Uganda was granted independence did not meet the basic aspirations of all the people of Uganda. It remains also that the original arrangement did not guarantee the peoples' authority. If anything, the Republican Constitution just took away peoples; authority and vested it under one man – The President. If this is the case, the necessary new arrangement which reflects the LINGUISTIC, CULTURAL, ETHNIC and SOCIAL DIVERSITY of the people of Uganda should be put in place.

It is only regrettable that Uganda is not yet a fully-fledged nation. Uganda is still a geographical expression; it is still a nation in the making. Once Uganda achieves nationhood it will be possible for a unitary constitution to be out in place.

I would totally agree with the Biblical verse of Jeremiah 10:23 when he stated:

> "...I well know, O Jehovah, that o earthling man his way does not belong; He does not belong to man who is walking even to direct his step..."

Afterword 4:

I PROTEST.

I want to state it clearly that what drove us to embark on armed struggle to oust Idi Amin-Dada from power was the quest for peace and security for all in our country. During Idi Amin-Dada's rule, there was peace and security for some Ugandans but lack if it for others. Those of us who came from Acholi, Lango and die-hard Uganda Peoples Congress (UPC) members were subjects of elimination as deemed expedient by the regime. Why should this be the case? The Almighty God created all of us to live our lives. Why should one, like Idi Amin-Dada think, we, his assumed opponents, should not live our lives, which is a God given right? No Nationalities in Uganda have gone through the kind of suffering us Acholi, Lango and die-hard members of UPC have gone through.

Anything that serves to remind us of this kind of suffering drives to speak up about such political design. We want peace and security for all Ugandans. We do not want any nationality in Uganda to go through the same suffering we have gone through. We are not ready to bargain about this because it is a God given right. We do not owe it to any human being that we should live or die. We owe it only to Jehovah[213] to live our lives and die because of sins we have inherited from the Biblical '...Adam and Eve...' and own property we have acquired through rightful means. Nothing short of this is what we have bargained for and we shall reject it with all the contempt it deserves.

Let us now look at the socio-economic, and cultural decay in '...Acholiland...' in particular, which has a bearing on Uganda as a whole today.

---

[213] Infers to the Hebrew name for God.

a. **Funerals and Burials**

I am now aging but when I was young, I used to take us, the Acholi, as very honest, trustworthy and not promiscuous. I am afraid this does not hold true among my people anymore. I discussed this problem with an intimate friend one day. He is from Butangire sub-county, Gulu District. In the course of our discussion, he cited two similar incidences which happened during the last funeral rites' performance he has attended. Given these two incidences, he told me that he will never again attend any last funeral rites in '...Acholiland...'.

We of the Acholi nationality, according to our culture, perform last funeral rites for our persons once they have died. We do this to celebrate their lives. This help to bring together members of the extended family of the dead persons and their friends so that they may know one another and inquire about the well-being of their families. For members of the extended family to meet and know one another are very important because it helps us to avoid marrying close relatives which is against our culture.

Members of some Christian religious denomination among us do not hold last funeral rites in the traditional way. They just hold final prayer instead after forty days when the deceased has been buried. And, it is now almost a normal practice among us that whenever a last funeral rite in the traditional way is being performed for the deceased, led by a priest of his or her religious denomination. The second day of the last funeral rites is then devoted to the performance of the funeral rites in the traditional way.

Last funeral rites in the traditional way among the Acholi nowadays are performed over the weekends. The attendees will begin to arrive at the venue on Fridays. That is when booths and tents of the attendees will take over the homestead of the deceased. Saturdays are devoted to prayer for the deceased

where applicable, and Sundays are when the traditional performance of the last funeral rites is performed.

Holding last funeral rites in the traditional way for the deceased elderly persons is an expensive undertaking because of eating, and excessive drinking involved during the occasion. And, as a consequence, some kind of fund raising is done among members of the extended family concerned; they have to donate either money or animals to be slaughtered for the occasions. Hence, several bulls and goats are slaughtered depending on the economic wellbeing of the extended family concerned. And, all sorts of drinks are consumed during the occasions leading to high level of drunkenness among the attendants.

Preparation for performing the last funeral rites in the traditional way to begin with involves the formation of an '...*Organising Committee*...' by members of the extended family concerned. It is the '...*Organising Committee*...' who will draw the budget for the occasion and work out how to implement the budget. The '...*Organising Committee*...' will send invitations to all members of the extended family, and where applicable request them for the contribution each is expected to come up with. Notable among those invited are the mothers-in-law of the extended family of the deceased, and the married daughters of the extended family of the deceased who are expected of course to come for the occasions with their husbands. The mothers-in-law invited usually know what is expected of them. The married daughters of the extended family on the on the other hand will be informed about the contribution that their husbands should make for the occasion.

b. **Funeral Attendants**

During the performance of the last funeral rites, it is a norm among the attendants to start a funeral song before one greets an acquaintance one has met. The acquaintance will then join in the singing after which they will exchange greetings. In the course of performing last funeral rites in the traditional way, the attendants dance what is known as '...*myel lyel...*' (funeral dance). It is a peculiar Acholi dance meant for the occasion. In the dance, adult male dancers wear head gears adorned with beautiful ostrich feathers holding shields in their left hand and spears in their right hands and their bodies at times decorated for the occasion and with their horns hung on a string around their necks.

They dance in a circular formation singing aloud funeral songs. The funeral songs are lamentations, odes, praise songs, or songs of thanks to the Almighty God for having removed the deceased from among his people, if the deceased was a wicked person. The arena for the last funeral rites' dance is always near the grave of the deceased.

The funeral songs are always accompanied by appropriate drumming for the occasion with additional sounds from two calabashes rubbed against a smooth dry log of a tree.

The drummers and those rubbing the two calabashes on the smooth dry log of a tree as part of the orchestra are always at the centre of the arena. The funeral dance is normally performed during the day time and goes on until late evening after which the dancers will withdraw to dance in front of their respective booths or tents if they are still in the mood for dancing.

Normally, at the end of any funeral song during the day time, male dancers may break the circular formation; run a mock to perform mock-fights with shield and spears in their hands in position for facing an adversary. They perform mock-fights, blow their horns, and cite poetry about themselves. The wives of those performing mock-fight will join their husbands and yodel in appreciation of what their husbands are doing.

I recall seeing white colonial administrators and members of their families coming to our village at Keyo to watch the dance whenever it was taking place there. The funeral dance would

amuse them a great deal especially when some male dance at the end of the funeral song break the circular formation to go and perform mock-fights with their imaginary enemies, blow their horns and cite brief poetry about who they are and their wives yodel in appreciation, and praising them. They would take photographs as they fancied and leave for Gulu Town, about 17 kilometres away late in the evening in their vehicles.

At dawn of the following morning on a Sunday, all attendants of the last funeral rites will assemble once more at the arena. They will sing three war-songs aloud accompanied by appropriate drumming. The three war-songs are to bid farewell to the soul of the deceased and straws are finally cast in unison towards the West where the sun sets. All attending will say:

"...let the setting sun take him/her for good..."!!

This will be repeated three times for a man and four times for a woman, as a finale of the last funeral rites of the departed soul.

During Sunday morning, mothers-in-laws take dishes of various foods they have prepared, drinks they have brought and even live animals like goats they have brought for the occasion in a given house. Members of the '...*Organising Committee*...' for the last funeral rites together with elders will examine what the various mothers-in-laws have brought. The mother-in-law who has out-performed other mothers-in-laws in her efforts will be ascertained and she will be rewarded accordingly. She will be given a bull or its equivalent of the three bull goats, she will be given several dishes which she will eat with those who accompanied her for the funeral, and she will be given assortments of drinks which they will drink. Last but not least she will be given appropriates amount of money which she will distribute among those who accompanied her for the last funeral rites. The bull she was given will be slaughtered consumed and some meat will be taken home by her entourage.

Towards noon, all the daughters of the extended family will assemble at a given place with their husbands in tow. Their husbands will be called in turn to give their contributions that have brought for the *'...burial...'* of the elderly person. *'...Burial...'* here is to be taken in a figurative sense. The *'...Organising Committee...'* for the last funeral rite who has received the contribution from the sons-in-laws of the extended family will declare the total amount of money collected and the number of animals brought. The *'...Organising Committee...'* will also declare the son-in-law who has contributed the most, the second and the third.

During the collection of the contributions, every son-in-law will come forward when called upon to do so, citing the motto of his sub-clan and declare what he has brought as his contribution for the burial of the deceased with his wife in tow and she may yodel in appreciation to what her husband has done.

At this juncture, members of the *'...Organising Committee...'* will withdraw from the venue to go and make their reports to the elders leaving behind the married daughters of the extended family with their husbands. Shortly they will come back at the venue, ask for some able-bodies daughters to assist in carrying assortments of dishes, drinks, and bulls that have been offered to be eaten by the married daughters of the extended family and their husbands. The *'...Organising Committee...'* will of course convey thanks from the elders to the sons-in-law for the contributions they have made for the burial of the deceased and informed them about what they have been given to eat and drink.

The married daughters of the extended family with their husbands will eat the food given and, drink the drinks given. The bull the married daughters of the extended family have received will be slaughtered. Some of the meat will be prepared and eaten and the rest will be shared among the married daughters

of the extended family that have come to attend the last funeral rites of the deceased elderly person.

Organising the last funeral rites in the traditional way among the Acholi for the elderly deceased may be an expensive affair but it is a win-win situation. Whatever contribution any member of the extended family has made will be given back in kind such that the attendants go home in high spirit. This is the case because the contribution of everybody is recognised and reciprocated accordingly in turn and kind.

Holding the last funeral rites in a traditional way is a great reunion for members of the extended family of the deceased. During the occasion there are a lot of interactions among members of the extended family. Mother-in-laws take food and drinks to their sons-in-laws. Sons-in-law in turn take food to their mothers-in-law. They do this whenever they go to greet one another. Once a party has presented what they have brought to another party, they start a funeral song they fancy, and the other party will join them to sing it after which they would leave. This is what happens normally during the performance of the last funeral rites in a traditional way among the Acholi.

C. Modernity

Nowadays, last funeral rites dance is performed briefly as a formality in the afternoon. As soon as this is done, the Disco Music System takes over until dawn of the following morning. You are a no-body if you do not bring a Disco Music System during the last funeral rites of your Dad or Mum. And the numbers of Disco Music System may depend on whose last funeral rite is being performed. When the last funeral rite of Chief Binyi of Pagak, Lamogi was being performed, it is hard to tell how many Disco Music Systems were being operated by the various attendants of the occasion. The Disco Music System is more or less a symbol of prestige among my people nowadays whenever the last funeral rites are being performed.

When the Disco Music System starts oozing out its modern music, who will not be dancing is the arena especially when the attendants have become tipsy. There, you will see even elderly persons, with their walking sticks held high in the air dancing to the latest tune up to the extent of even outperforming the young folks. They will only cry of body aches at day break of the following morning.

The young folks will dance in the arena where the light is a bit dim to cater for their mischiefs. At dawn of the following morning, the Disco Music System will only stop playing to give room for the traditional finale of the last funeral rites. During the traditional finale if the last funeral rites as I have already explained before, the war songs will be sung, and straws cast towards the West by the dancers in unison as required either three times or four times according to the sex of the deceased; chanting:

"...let the setting sun take it for good!..."

will be repeated accordingly each time straws are being cast westwards, that is towards where the sun sets.

Some morning now, what will you find in the compound of the homesteads? In the extreme case, you will find empty sachets of Uganda Waragi and other related tribes and clans of spirits distilled in Uganda nowadays; dry gin and vodka. At the periphery of the homestead, you will find used condoms. You will have to organise a team that will move quickly throughout the compound of the homestead to remove used condoms least children will begin blowing them as balloons. This sight will shock you, but this is the reality of what happens at night during some last funeral rites of elderly persons in '...Acholiland...' nowadays.

We sit back and lament about how promiscuous we have become nowadays. We then ask ourselves, what has become of our morality? At least this is what my intimate friend saw in the two last funeral rites he had attended in Palaro sub-county and Butangira sub-county, Aswa county, all in the Gulu District, which is why he has resolved never again to attend any traditional last funeral rites in '...Acholiland...' whatsoever. In view of what he told me, I, too, is no longer proud of Acholi culture because I now have nothing, I can be proud of in terms of morality among my people. We Acholi can now indulge in any sorts of vices to the extent that you may not believe what you see or hear. I have not seen the kind of this sort of immorality when I was young.

d. Internal Displaced Camps [IDPs]

The culprit is the Internally Displaced Camps [IDPs][214] which were created all over '...Acholiland...' during the civil war which went on between the Uganda Peoples Defence Force (UPDF)[215] and the Lord's Resistance Army (LRA)[216] of Joseph Kony for about twenty years in '...Acholiland...'. At the beginning of the civil war Acholi were uprooted from their homes and herded like cattle into IDPs. The IDPs, if anything was the German NAZI-like concentration camps of the modern era in disguised. The act of creating them was an act of war crime. Though on the face of it one would think it was humane to do that because that was the

---

[214] This was a designer NRA-regime policy of forcibly putting a population of 3 million Acholi people into internment camps. According to Gen. Yoweri Museveni, was to deny rebels access to the population and starve both of food.

[215] Came into existence in 1987 after Mr Yoweri Kaguta Museveni had been in power for 1 year.

[216] Came into existence in 1987 after the collapse or crushing of the Ms Alice Auma Lakwena's Holy Spirit Movement (HSM), which had resisted the NRA from 1986. The consequence was atrocities meted out to the Acholi people, which saw the emergence of Mr Joseph Kony as its leader. Alice was recalled by the ancestors in January 2007.

only way civilians in '...*Acholiland*...' could be protected against the wrath of LRA.

But, the IDPs were not created for civilians in '...*Acholiland*...' only. UPDF in their cowardice always located them detaches at the centre of IDPs. In other words, civilians in '...*Acholiland*...' were being used as shields by UPDF against the LRA during the civil war. The creation of IDPs were not planned, it came all of a sudden because the President of Uganda, Mr Yoweri Kaguta Museveni, directed that they should be created because according to him live domestic animals among the Acholi were dangerous weapons in the armoury of LRA. As a consequence, there was no supply of food and provisions of healthcare at the beginning when these IDPs were being established.

The humanitarian Non-Government Organisations (NGO) moved there much later to supply food and provide healthcare which was always inadequate to begin with. Naturally, people who were herded into IDPs suffered hunger, lack of medical care and sickness that overcrowding always creates. They whole world kept quiet. It was only much later that the world realised the suffering of the people of Acholi in IDPs. The death rate especially among children and the elderly persons was very high. All this was in the name of protecting people from the excesses of LRA.

At the same time, our culture was being fought and undermined in the IDPs by UPDF as if it was its major mission to do so. Once, Acholi were in IDPs, children began sharing limited spaces with their parents something which was contrary to our culture. And, at night, what was going on between a man and his wife was being heard and seen by their children. This was not possible under a normal setup in Acholi homes in the past whereby children of age did not sleep together with their parents in the same hut. Young boys normally slept in their own hut known as '...*otogo*...' Young girls who were of age slept together with the elderly relatives in the home; with aunties or grannies in separate huts.

The kind of sexual immorality youths in '...Acholiland...' nowadays are indulging themselves in is no longer the normal sexual intercourse but extraordinary sexual acts of even homosexuality which was brought in '...Acholiland...' by the National Resistance Army (NRA)[217]/UPDF The intimate friend I have mentioned elsewhere before told me that in one of the last funeral rites he attended in Palaro sub-county, Aswa county, Gulu District young men lined up to have sexual intercourse in turn with a tipsy young woman by the front or homosexually. A young man had to state his preference and had a go at it.

He told me that a similar incidence took place during another last funeral rite which took place later in Bungatiro sub-county, Aswa county, Gulu District. This incidence took place just near Bungatiro Central Primary School. Here again some errant youths rounded up another tipsy young woman, lined up and has sexual intercourse with her by the front and homosexually. Because of these two incidences, my intimate friend has resolved not to attend any traditional last funeral rites in '...Acholiland...'

These behaviours by our young men had a precedent. During the civil war as I have already mentioned, some Uganda Peoples Defence Forces (UPDF)[218] soldiers were known to have had homosexual intercourse with married men in front of their wives and children. This was of course either to break the will of the Acholi from supporting the Lord's Resistance Army (LRA) if at all they were doing so or to demonstrate their manhood that they had defeated Acholi. After such humiliation, such victims were known to have dutifully committed suicide. The few victims that did not commit suicide are suffering silently with whatever

---

[217] The name of the Armed Force of Mr Yoweri Kaguta Museveni before seizing power in 1986; and thereafter was renamed the UPDF - Ibid 191

[218] The drug used to stem the debilitating effect of the HIV virus allowing a modicum of functionality to the affected

injuries they attained during their humiliation. They have nowhere to go for redress. Uganda Mass Media reported exhaustively about such happenings. Such acts took place under command of Major General David Tinyefunza ala Sejusa[219].

During the civil war, housewives and young girls were at times forcibly detained by UPDF in their detaches whereby they were sexually abused by UPDF soldiers who had HIV[220]. After a short while those women and young girls who were detained in military detaches passed on due to HIV they had acquired from UPDF soldiers and later on their husbands passed on too. By this time there was no **Anti-Retroviral [ARV]**[221] drugs yet, no one affected with HIV could live with it for fairly long time. The son of my late brother, Mr John Okoya, by the name of Acaye suffered this kind of fate at Pabbo sub-county, Kilak county, Amuru District.

Some young girls and women however had consensual sexual intercourse with UPDF soldiers infected with HIV, as a consequence they infected many other young men and passed on later. HIV therefore was used as a biological weapon during the civil war against Acholi by NRM government and UPDF to exterminate Acholi. This explained why '...*Acholiland...*' now has the second highest level of HIV incidences after the Toro sub-region in Uganda. In the latest Ministry of Health Statistics releases towards the end of 2014, while the national average of HIV incidences statistics at 7.3%, the rate of HIV incidences in Gulu stands at 8.3%, which as above national average.

Sexual immorality is an abomination when it takes place between both married and unmarried couples. And the punishment for both fornication and adultery among the Jews of the Old Testament was death by stoning for both offenders.

---

[219] In 2013 as head of the Military Intelligence protested the NRA-behaviour towards the population, was removed from the military and started a quasi-anti-NRA political organisation.
[220] Human Immunodeficiency Virus (HIV) is a vicious virus that attacks the immune system, and can kill infected people if it's left untreated.
[221] Ibid 221

Homosexuality is a great abomination it is not a human right as others claim it to be. If it was a human right, the Almighty God could not have destroyed Sodom and Gomorrah. Homosexuality is a satanic act and it was not sanctified at any given time or place by the Almighty God; Jehovah.

Those who introduced homosexuality in Acholi and in the modern era did this to demonstrate their manhood, and also to destroy our culture because they knew that once introduced, youths in '...*Acholiland*...' will follow their examples by indulging themselves in it. Here, I wish to state that they have achieved their objective. The onus is now upon us to banish this satanic practice from our midst because it's against our culture.

During the civil war between the LRA and UPDF for twenty years in '...*Acholiland*...', we were not in control of our culture anymore. We were just on the run, minding just about our lives. This was when those who came to destroy our culture were busy at it. They knew that we are proud of our culture and it is what makes us stand apart from other Ugandans. Hence, one of their mission was to destroy these very sources of our pride; our culture, if possible.

Despite what has already happened, we have no option but to stand up and revive our culture. We have to re-examine critically our culture. Are there some practices which, we must now discard from our culture? Answering this question candidly calls for collective efforts from all of us as Acholi.

However, if I could have my way, the practice of brushing our teeth with fine white sand among Acholi must now cease. It has outlived its usefulness since it ends up in the same time to destroy our teeth altogether. Another thing is that, to avoid immoral sexual intercourse that takes place late at night during the performance of last funeral rite, it would be prudent for us to perform rites during day time only. We should not allow it to extend at night. And we should banish the Disco Music System from performance of last funeral rites. We should go back to our traditional ways of performing last funeral rites. We should go back to singing funeral songs and dancing funeral dances as our ancestors used to do. This at the same time would help in reviving our culture as well.

We have also to take note of the fact that some soldiers of the UPDF to destroy our culture have used satanic practices. The implication of this is that we have to counter these satanic practices by embracing Christianity much as we try to revive our culture. We have to move away from being nominal Christians and become Christian ministers.

e. Coca Plants[222]

Another thing which those of us who fought against Idi Amin-Dada to oust him from power, and did not bargain for, was the introduction of Coca Plants in Uganda. Is Coca Plant a cash crop? How good is it? Why should one introduce it in '...*Acholiland*...' above all?

I wish to inform my fellow countrymen and the world at large that Coca Plants are now rampant in '...*Acholiland*...'; especially in the Districts of Gulu, Nwoya and Amuru.

I have taken trouble to investigate how Coca plants have been introduced in '...*Acholiland*...'. The chorus of answers I received were that, they were introduced by the UPDF, that is, our national army during the civil war. According to the information I have gathered from three Districts already mentioned, some UPDF soldiers went about sowing seeds of Coca Plants in '...*Acholiland*...' wherever they went during the civil war.

Why? No one can tell for certain. I am of the view however that, Coca Plants were introduced as a long-term weapon for the continued aggression against Acholi people through other means. We all know how bad cocaine is for human consumption. Cocaine

---

[222] Coca is any of the four cultivated plants in the family Erythroxylaceae, native to the western South America.

is too good for the destruction of human lives. Those who have introduced Coca Plants in '...*Acholiland*...' are targeting our youths in the long-term. They want to destroy our youths in the long run once. The youths have developed the habit of consuming cocaine and have become addicted to it.

Youths the world over as we well know are the vitality of any nation. As a silent weapon, consumption of cocaine will catch up for sure among our youth, and that will be when our country will become ungovernable as some Latin American countries like Colombia and Mexico today.

And there is a conspiracy of silence about the presence of Coca Plants in Uganda and more so in '...*Acholiland*...' What is Uganda Community Police doing about it? How about the Uganda government's Internal Security Organisation [ISO]? With Coca Plants rampant in '...*Acholiland*...', what will be the fate of Uganda as a whole? How about the fate of our neighbouring countries and the fate of African countries as a whole?

I know that Coca Plants are not indigenous plants of Uganda. Can any botanist in any of our universities prove me wrong? Do we need Coca Plants in Uganda? It is now so sad to note that who-so-ever is in need of cocaine now does not have to go up to South America to get it. He or she must come to Uganda; a least expected place for it. He or she can come and setup secretly a Laboratory for manufacturing cocaine from leaves of Coca Plants in '...*Acholiland*...'

The origin of Coca Plants is South America that the Incas grew the Coca Plants whose leaves contain cocaine. Drug Barons who smuggle cocaine all over the world are mainly from South American countries; notably Colombia and Mexico. Are those Drug Barons, if I may ask, ones who have introduced Coca Plants in Uganda? And, can we now say for certain that those Ugandans who were executed in China for taking cocaine there got it from Uganda or they got it from some South American countries? Do we now have Laboratories for manufacturing cocaine in Uganda for export!!, one wonders!!

I write appealing to organisations and countries concerned about control of dangerous drugs like cocaine in the world to help us eradicate Coca Plants from our midst in Uganda. I appeal to them to help us do so before consumption of cocaine catches up with our youths in '...Acholiland...' and in Uganda as a whole. This is my 'SOS' (Save Our Soul)!! Twelve more Ugandans are, as I write are on death row in China for having taken large quantity of cocaine to China. Many more Ugandans are in jail in China facing similar charges of taking cocaine to China. How many Ugandans are we going to lose needlessly in China for taking cocaine there?

> On 18th February 2015, it was widely reported in our Newspapers that Rwandese Security arrested an individual who boarded a plane in Entebbe International Airport, upon landing in Kigali, for carrying several kilos of cocaine.

With Coca Plants rampant in '...Acholiland...' some of our youth who smoke marijuana are already experimenting with consuming seeds of Coca Plants in order to get '...high...' One youth confided to me that sewing three seeding of Coca Plants is enough to enable one to become 'high'. Hence, our youths who are consumers of marijuana are now graduating to the consumption of seeds of Coca Plants. Some youths have confided to me that some Asian shopkeepers in Gulu Town are now known to be selling seeds of Coca Plant to youth who are addicted to marijuana.

A point in case is what took place in Alelele Primary School, Alero sub-county, Nwoya District.

> On 7th October 2014, Radio Mega 102 FM, Gulu, came out with a newscast about a pupil of the Primary

School who took seeds of unknown weeds to school and gave it to his fellow pupil to sew them.

It seems the pupil who sewed them sewed one too many and the result was disastrous. He nearly died of this. The radio newscast went to state that the seeds of the unknown weeds were collected by the errant pupil from Olwoo village.

This newscast went on to state that the school authority was so much concerned about the incident. They reported the matter to the parents of the errant pupil and advised them to uproot the weeds in their village. Just uprooting the weeds mark you! Not uprooting and burning them altogether! I am convinced beyond reasonable doubt the pupil chew seeds of Coca Plants before taking it to the school. Radio Mega 102 FM Gulu, did not report the whole truth. The Radio could have called a spade a spade. Whom was it protecting? Some of our youths are now experimenting with sewing Coca Plants seeds in order to get 'high'. To mess up some of their friends, some youths have developed the habit of slipping a seed of Coca plant in pairs of shoes of their colleagues. The innocent fellow will put on his pair of shoes without suspecting any foul-play and in the end; he will get 'high' without knowing the root cause of his malaise. One youth who operates a motor bike taxi confided to me that it is the sewing of Coca Plant seeds that is causing a lot of motor accidents among the youth operating motor bike taxis. It is regrettable that people in '...*Acholiland*...' are being duped to grow Coca Plants in their homesteads under mistaken belief that the extracts from their leaves help fight poultry epidemic. Yet in reality, they are toying with real danger.

The government of Uganda is quiet about the existence of Coca Plants in Uganda, and the fact that some of our youths are now sewing its seeds in order to get '...*high*...' Given the intensity of the government's intelligence network, our President, Mr Yoweri Kaguta Museveni, can even read a report about a drop of a pin in my village at Keyo. Why it is than

Uganda government has not yet embarked on eradication of Coca Plant in Uganda? Does Uganda Government approve the introduction and growing of Coca Plants in our country? If so why? It is long overdue that Uganda government must come out with a law banishing the introduction and growing of Coca Plants in Uganda altogether. Uganda government should spell out a deterrent penalty for introduction and growing of Coca Plant in Uganda. A Police Department should be created specifically for the eradication of these plants from Uganda which should involve uprooting and burning there wherever they are being grown. Some youths in Koch sub-county, Nwoya District is known to be growing Coca Plant on a semi commercial level. They harvest ten to twenty kilos of Coca Plants seeds for sale to dealers who come from Kampala. I am afraid we are really in for it – a mode of ethnic cleansing.

f. Bonfire and Granaries

What drove us to fight and oust Idi Amin-Dada from power was the quest for peace and security for all Ugandans as I have stated before.

After ousting Idi Amin-Dada from power, we expected to have peace and security for our lives and property. In '...Acholiland...' today we keep on telling ourselves that there is peace and security with the departure of Mr Joseph Kony and his Lord's Resistance Army (LRA) from '...Acholiland...' But the true peace and true security I knew as I was growing up in '...Acholiland...' is peace and security with all its symbols; notably making of bonfires at night at the centre of our homes and the existence of granaries in our homesteads. It is true that we can make bonfires at night at the centre of our homes but most of our homes now lack granaries. The existence of granaries in every homestead and the making of bonfires at night whenever the weather permits at the centre of each homestead are symbols of true peace and true security as a norm.

During the civil war, making bonfire at the centre of the homestead at night whenever the weather permitted was prohibited. This was because of LRA that would come and round up all those seated around the bonfires and take them away into captivity. The bonfires made at the centre of our homestead were where we got informal education from the feet of our wise elders. They would teach us what children ought to know as far as our culture and morality was concerned.

Bonfires are made at the centre of our homestead during peace time when the weather permits. We make them symbolising peace and security prevailing in our community, and '...Acholiland...' as a whole.

Granaries too are symbols of food security when full of dry food. In the past, granaries were also built on top of graves of elderly persons. Shadows of granaries therefore used to be revered for giving peaceful rest to souls of departed elders.

I regret to state that so far, we have failed to get any replacement of granaries for storage of dry food stuff. We cannot let go these vital structures from our homestead given the practical and symbolic roles they play in our culture and community. Either we have them, or we are no longer Acholi people without them. We should not fear defending our culture. We must bring back granaries in our homesteads, and we must work hard to ensure that no one steals dry food stored in them as it used to be in the past.

With the civil war, which went on between the Uganda Peoples Defence Force (UPDF) and the LRA in '...Acholiland...', I have learnt that culture is something that should be guarded jealously and continuously least it could be eroded as it is the case now with ours. During the civil war, sanctity of granaries was being abused at will by the LRA, and those of like mind. Nowadays, criminal elements among us are doing the same. We must fight these criminals and defeat them so that we may restore the sanctity of granaries as it used to be in the past.

Granaries used to be structures in our homes which used to guide us to be honest and trustworthy. No one used to open and enter granaries of any other person. If one wants anything from them, he or she has to ask the owner who will give him or her, what he or she wants from any granary. It was an abomination in our culture for anyone to open and enter granaries that do not belong to him or her under whatever pretext. If you are found opening and entering into any granary of someone else without his or her permission, the penalty was you will bring a lamb which will be slaughtered by elders to sanctify it, and you will be obliged to return what you have stolen from that granary; and promise never to steal again from any granary which does not belong to you. This is our culture pure and simple.

Respect for sanctity of granaries may look simple and childish for someone who is a stranger in '...*Acholiland*...' But, the sanctity of granaries was paramount in our culture; this was how we used to maintain self-discipline, honesty, and trustworthiness for every one of us. Respect for sanctity of granaries must be brought back if we want to both please and live as our ancestors used to live their lives. There is no way out or else we shall get lost to our detriment as it now seems to be the case. Let us reclaim back our culture with all the seriousness it deserves!

Granaries are structures in which dry food is stored. They are normally built in Acholi homestead for that purpose. There are three types of granaries which were normally built in '...*Acholiland*...' First, we have ordinary granaries whose roofs are opened by the use of forked pole of about three metres long or so. Second, we have grand granaries known as '...*goga*...' that are built in such a way that part of it, all round the roofs, remain open for climbing in and out of them. So, to climb in and out of '...*goga*...' one does not need forked poles known as '...*layibi*...' for opening the roofs as in the case with ordinary granaries. '...*Goga*...' normally stores three to six times the amount of dry food that can be stored in ordinary granary. The

last type of granary is known as '...*phut*...' They are built of clay and straws. They have roofs that are opened with forked poles. This type of granary is used for storage of '...*sim sim*...' and other seed crops.

Granaries were structures we used to have in every homestead in '...Acholiland...' before the twenty-year civil war that went on between UPDF and LRA for storage of dry food. The various types of dry food stored in granaries are generally cereals like millet, sorghum, rice, maize, and other seed crops like '...*sim sim*...', peas, pigeon peas, yams, and pumpkins among others. That was in the past. As of now, granaries are no longer a common sight in every homestead of '...Acholiland...' Why? Because we fear that, whatever dry food you store in granaries is no longer yours.

How has this come about? This is one of the LRA legacies that have refused to go away much as the LRA is no longer here in '...Acholiland...' During the twenty-year civil war, LRA fighters used to empty granaries of their contents at will in search of food. With the departure of the LRA from '...Acholiland...', criminals among us have continued to wreak havoc. We Acholi have not yet taken a stand to fight and defeat these criminals in order to guarantee security of dry food in our granaries. The challenge we have in '...Acholiland...' today is the restoration of granaries in every homestead and guard them once restored to ensure that no one steals from them as it used to be in the past. Fearing to store dry food in granaries is one thing but guarding jealously against theft from them and punishing those found stealing from them is another thing.

As far as Acholi culture is concerned granaries in our homestead and the making of bonfires at the centre of our homestead at night whenever the weather permits are symbols of true peace and security. One cannot make bonfires at the centre of his home during war time, least your enemies may come, and wipe out the entire members of the family around bonfires of the day.

g. Alcoholism.

This has paved the way for alcoholism among the Acholi and is causing impotence among able-bodied males leading to collapse of happy marriages.

Since time immemorial, '...*Latiina*...'[223] is known to have invented the science of brewing millet beer known as '...*kwete*...' among the Acholi. She is known to have collected remains of dry millet bread, pounded it with mortar, soaked it in water, and added flour of millet that has germinated (yeast) and left the solution to ferment. After a day or so, it became a delicious drink that could make one get drunk. '...*Latiina*...' sieved it and begun drinking it. This delicious drink could make the spirit of a tired soul to rest so peacefully when he or she has consumed it. '...*Latiina*...' is known to have taken some of this delicious drink to her clan chief. And this is what led to her undoing.

The clan chief drank it and became drunk and slept peacefully thereafter. His people tried to wake him up in vain. Remember his people were seeing for the first time someone failing to wake up because he was under the influence of alcohol. They assumed that '...*Latiina*...' had poisoned their clan chief, and that he was destined to die. They in rage decided to kill '...*Latiina*...' because they assumed that their chief was going to die of what he drank.

However, after some time, the chief woke up sane and sound. He asked for '...*Latiina*...' only to be told that they had already killed '...*Latiina*...' for offering him the drink they thought was going to kill him. The chief was furious at what they did. He told his subjects that '...*Latiina*...' has given him a delicious

---

[223] Inference to Acholi specific mythology

drink which enabled him to enjoy his sleep more than he has ever done before. She therefore did not deserve to die for that. All the same, the chief's appreciation of what '...Latiina...' did for him was one too late! '...Latiina...' was already dead! Acholi always remind themselves about the death of '...Latiina...'! Hence, much as we have to be generous, we must be careful as we go about it or else, we may be misunderstood and die of it like '...Latiina...'.

From then on, others improved on the quality of the delicious drink that '...Latiina...' first brew. They ground millet, added a bit of water to the millet flour, and allowed the solution to ferment until sour. Once it has fermented, it is roasted and sun-dried. To brew '...kwete...' from dried, roasted fermented milled flour known as '...moko kong'o...' is soaked in appropriate quantity of water then appropriate quantity of fermented millet flour is added in it and left to brew. After a day or so, our millet beer is ready to be sieved for drinking. The longer it is brewed the stronger it is. '...Kwete...' is the alcoholic drink Acholi have been drinking since time immemorial.

However, '...kwete...' was consumed by adult married men in measured quantity. It was consumed by married adult males because they were supposed to be responsible enough to control themselves under influence of alcoholic drinks. They did not drink to get drunk but to drink to enjoy their leisure time. Drinking '...kwete...' among them was not an everyday affair, it was drunk only when the occasion merited it. It may be brewed for communal digging, for last funeral rites or for marriage occasion.

Young men among the Acholi were not known for drinking mature '...kwete...' that may make one get drunk. It was only married adult males who drank mature '...kwete...'. If young men have to have a taste of '...kwete...' they drunk sweet '...kwete...', that is 'kwete' that has not yet over matured with high alcoholic content in it. I recall one day we drank sweet

'...*kwete*...' with other young men. The experience we got out of it was not good. The sweet '...*kwete*...', once it matured in our stomachs caused us to belch with tears in our eyes and pain in our nostrils. As a result, from then onwards, I shunned drinking '...*kwete*...' at any level of maturity.

'...*Kwete*...' as a traditional alcoholic drink was drunk by married adult men. Women just drunk a little bit with modesty. In a communal farming/digging, once youth have finished helping someone who has called them to open up a new field, they would just eat the various dishes offered and go away to take care of their other businesses. It was their fathers and uncles that would come to drink the '...*kwete*...'; for the occasion. They would take their time consuming the '...*kwete*...' which was brewed, sing, and dance traditional dance. And, they knew how to drink. It was a disgrace to drink until one is a nuisance to others. Once someone is drunk, he will go, sleep, and wake up later when he is sober.

When the Arabs and their Nubian guides began frequenting '...*Acholiland*...' during the era of slave trade and barter trade, they were known to have introduced the science of distilling '...*waragi*...' (War Gins)[224] among the Acholi. They were consuming measured quantity of '...*waragi*...' to pass their leisure time. This may sound contradictory that it was the Muslims who introduced the distillation and consumption of spirits in Uganda. Since Islam is opposed to drinking of alcohol. But, believe me, the Arabs and their Nubian guides were the ones who introduced the vice in Uganda. They did it, but they knew how to drink, since they consumed only measured quantity for a given day to enable them to enjoy their leisure time.

---

[224] In later years the name 'Waragi' was that officially distilled by East African Distilleries (U) Ltd. To differentiate the locally distilled, the local distillers then changed the name to '...*arege*...'. The difference is that the '...*arege*...' alcohol content varies according to expertise of the distillers. It's this '...*arege*...' that is a problem in '...*Acholiland*...'

With time, the Acholi also started aping them. It was our elderly men who began drinking spirit but they too like the Arabs and their Nubian guides knew how to drink because they used to drink measured quantity of '...*waragi*...' They did not drink to get drunk but drank to pass their leisure time too, if the occasion permitted it. Old women, the grannies, were the ones who used to distil '...*waragi*...' in '...*Acholiland*...' at the beginning once the science of distillation was mastered from the Arabs and their Nubian guides. In each distillation, an old woman may get about three to five litres of '...*waragi*...' which she would seal securely in an earthen jar. Any elder in need of it would part with a sizeable billy goat in exchange. He will then deposit this jar full of '...*waragi*...' in the hut of his favourite wife. Mark you most of the Acholi elders of long ago were polygamists.

When a friend or friends pay such an elder a visit, he would take them in the hut of his favourite wife where the jar of '...*waragi*...' is kept. He would ask his favourite wife to produce the far and he would open it. He will pour some '...*waragi*...' in a small calabash and drink it the he would invite his guests to do the same in turn. They may repeat the exercise just once again, and then he would request his wife to return the jar for safe custody until another occasion.

With everyone having taken his share, the host and his guests will now chat with one another. At this juncture, the guests may make known the subject of their visits to their host, and the host will respond accordingly to each of the subject where possible.

Later they would continue chatting with one another and may take a meal together, and thereafter, when all the business has been exhausted, the guests would depart for the irrespective homes. Acholi elders of long ago knew how to drink alcohol. They did not consume alcohol in order to get drunk but drank to enjoy their leisure time.

With advent of colonialism in Uganda, Acholi youths began joining the colonial armed forces- **Kings African Rifles (KAR)**[225].

In the call of their duties, particularly for those who served in the KAR, they travelled far and wide visiting and living in various urban centres of East Africa and even beyond. They learnt the habit of drinking until one is drunk. When they got their short or long leave, they would come home, and they brought this new life style in '...Acholiland...' While on leave, they would move about visiting their relatives and would drink beyond their optimum measure for enjoying leisure time. If relatives come to visit them, they would buy for them alcoholic drinks be it '...kwete...' or '...waragi...' Since they had money and played host most of the time. Elders did not gather enough courage to tell them off about this new life style. All in all, our colonial soldiers, policemen and warders, during their holidays in the respective villages, passed their leisure time drinking to the youths who accompanied them to drinking places.

Alcoholism began making inroads in '...Acholiland...' to the extent never known before. It became more or less an acceptable lifestyle. I am not saying that all colonial soldiers, policemen, and warders used to drink. They were exception; some were teetotallers! And despite this new life style they have acquired during their call-off duties, they were very responsible persons. They paid dowries for wives of their brothers where necessary apart from paying their own dowries, a role that only fathers used to pay among the Acholi. They too were development agents. In the course of their duties, they saw the importance of sending their kith and kin to school to promote education. I am a product of such gestures and I am too grateful for it. My father could ill-afford to pay my school fees but my elder brother, the late Mr John Okoya who was in KAR had to foot the school fees for my education. Any Acholi youths who was in the colonial armed forces and was not supporting some of his kin and kith in school was a nobody!

---

[225] Ibids 70

But one would say in strict confidence that the majority of Acholi youths who ventured into joining the colonial armed forces did not know how to drink since most of them drank until they became drunk. Was this an occupational hazard? No one can tell for certain. But it was this new life style which they brought home and the villager's copied from them. Did they pick this life style in town slums where the army garrisons were situated, and used to frequent? The colonial army officers knew how to drink; they drank to pass time or enjoy their leisure time. They knew that taking too much alcohol is harmful to human life. When it came to taking spirits; they took it in tots and rarely neat but mixed with bitter lemons or tonics. Beer is taken in standard drink units which their body can support not beyond with known alcohol content in it. It was common to see a white man spectating a Rugby match for example taking just one bottle of beer during the whole match! They did not drink to get drunk but rank to pass leisure time or for the purpose of sharpening their appetite before a meal.

During Idi Amin-Dada's regime we the Acholi passed through a very difficult time that we had never known before. Many among us resorted to heavy drinking in order to forget the unprecedented suffering they were going through. But this too much consumption of alcohol did not solve any of the problems. If anything, it added more to their suffering subjecting them to poverty and alcoholism. Idi Amin-Dada's regime came to pass but alcoholism among my people continued and gained epidemic proportion during the twenty-year civil war which took place in '...Acholiland...' between the Uganda Peoples Defence Force (UPDF)[226] and Mr Joseph Kony's Lord's Resistance Army (LRA)[227].

With most of the people locked up in IDPs[228], the occupants of the camps had little work to do and spent most of their leisure

---

[226] Ibid 215
[227] Ibid 214
[228] Ibid 216

times drinking alcohol. This they did it to forget the suffering they were going through, but alcoholism was making deeper inroads in '...*Acholiland*...'. Was this one of the reasons for herding Acholi into IDPs? In the IDPs the Acholi drank and made children, this was their major preoccupation therein? But there were also very high rates of death among young children, and the elderly persons at the beginning of IDPs.

Even when the twenty-year civil war between UPDF and LRA came to an end in '...*Acholiland*...' consumption of alcohol especially spirits continued harming the Acholi in earnest. In this case, the momentum was maintained through constant and excessive supply of spirits in '...*Acholiland*...' from Southern and Western Regions of Uganda. '...*Acholiland*...' became a prime market for spirits distilled from southern and western regions of Uganda. Crude spirits of all sorts like '...*ofa muntu*...' and '...*science waragi*...' from western region were distilled especially to be supplied to '...*Acholiland*...' With NRA/M-government economic policy of liberalisation. Many distillers sprung up in Uganda. In the past we knew only of one distiller of spirits in Uganda – this is East African Distilleries (U) Ltd that distils Uganda Waragi.

We now have dozens of distillers belonging mainly to Asians turning out all sorts of clans and tribes of spirits presented to consumers in sachets at a highly affordable price. Much as people in '...*Acholiland*...' are busy consuming these various kinds '...*waragi*...', gins and vodka, they are taking tolls in their lives. Uganda government has not come up with any programme to check on the excessive consumption of alcohol among Ugandans especially in '...*Acholiland*...' The World Health Organisation [WHO] has sounded a warning that consumption of alcohol harming Ugandans is too high in average per individual per year to no avail!

I am now grateful at least that some local leaders in '...*Acholiland*...' especially the Kitgum District have started

banishing sales of alcohol in sachets and import of crude '...*waragi*...' in jerry cans from Southern and Western Regions of Uganda to their districts by coming up with a bye-law to that effect. This is a step in the right direction however late it may be. It is better late than never!

However, despite the bold steps, the local authorities and traditional leaders in Kitgum Districts have taken to come up with the bye-law that banishes the sachets and crude '...*waragi*...' from southern and western regions of Uganda, other districts of '...*Acholiland*...' have not yet followed suit. It is as to note thus fact. Why are we elsewhere burying our heads in the sand as if nothing harmful is happening to the lives of our youths who are the majority of consumers of these evil spirits.

Saturation of market in '...*Acholiland*...' with all sorts of spirits has been more or less official policy with NRA/M government stamp all over it, to subject Ugandans in '...*Acholiland*...' to extreme alcoholism. When most people in '...*Acholiland*...' are alcoholic, the framers of this kind of economic policy shall have achieved their objective of destroying us through alcoholism. Any caring government in the world could have made an effort to fight alcoholism in her country. When the former President of Zambia, Dr Kenneth Kaunda[229] saw the extent to which Zambians were drinking alcohol (beer), he cried during a public rally, to demonstrate his revulsion. He told his nation that he was not taking delight in leading a country of drunkards! He appealed to his people to desist from too much consumption of alcohol. This was the feeling of a caring President. In Uganda, it seems that feeling about alcoholism among Ugandans as far as our political leaders are concerned is the reverse of what President Kenneth Kaunda did! But former President Kenneth Kaunda was complaining about excessive consumption of beer among his people. He was not complaining about excessive consumption of spirits. Here in Uganda we are

---

[229] famously referred to as 'KK'.

complaining about excessive consumption of spirits not beer. In developed countries, to keep their workers happy, the government subject them to a lot of consumption of beer by making it very much affordable to them. Yet our longest serving President to date[230], that is over 30 years, Mr Yoweri Kaguta Museveni is a teetotaller.

In summary as far as the political history of Uganda is concerned, from 1971 up to 1979, when Idi Amin-Dada was ruling Uganda, we Acholi did not have peace and security. This disrupted socio-economic development in '...Acholiland...' causing, if anything under-development subjecting our people to abject poverty which we are still wallowing in. Those of us who happened to be elites or who were serving in armed forces, particularly in the Uganda Army were subjects of elimination when deemed expedient by Idi Amin-Dada. We enjoyed a brief spell of peace and security from 1979 up to 1985 after the ouster of Idi Amin-Dada from power.

However, when NRA/M assumed power in 1986, there was a twenty-year civil way in '...Acholiland...' between the UPDF and the LRA of Joseph Kony. In ensuring civil war, we lost a lot of lives, property, and time for development. When the NRA stepped in '...Acholiland...', their military officers were called 'commanders'. It was Commander Dr Warren Kizza Besigye-Kifefe[231] who commanded the first contingent of NRA who ventured into '...Acholiland...' once NRA/M captured power on 26th January 1986 from Okellos. In Lamogi sub-county headquarter at Pyela, Pagak, NRA killed 27 civilians in cold blood without any provocation whatsoever. Nothing was done about

---

[230] Idi Amin-Dada served only 8 years; and Dr Apollo Milton Obote's two Presidential terms totalling 10 years and 4 years as Executive Prime Minister, thus only 14 years.

[231] Later as a decorated military 'Colonel' served as the NRA Chief Political Commissar and Minister of Internal Affairs under the NRA/M-regime; thereafter a presidential candidate against Gen. Yoweri Museveni and Leader of Agenda 21/Forum for Democratic Change (FDC).

this to date, by NRA/M government. The NRA soldiers who murdered the 27 civilians were not prosecuted up to now. Similar wanton killings of innocent civilians by NRA soldiers can be cited all over '...Acholiland...' in the name of revenge for what happened in Luwero Triangle during the 1981-1985 NRA bush war, much as there were also several wanton killings by LRA of civilians in '...Acholiland...'

h. Domestic wealth

Cattle and other domestic animals were either looted by LRA for food and by NRA as a means of depriving LRA fighters with food supply, subjecting Acholi later to an abject poverty after the civil war. I personally lost 38 herds of cattle to NRA during the civil war for which I have not yet been compensated as promised to the Acholi War Claimants Association by Uganda Government.

i. Immorality

Immorality in the form of prostitution and in the form of gay life style is here to stay with us once introduced by UPDF in '...Acholiland...' during the civil war. It is that we Acholi are now enjoying comparative peace and security with the departure of Joseph Kony's LRA from '...Acholiland...' However, most of the evils that were introduced in '...Acholiland...' by either NRA or LRA are still with us. Why should we Acholi be the subject of such suffering begging from Idi Amin-Dada era to date?

j. Procreation

Many young women in '...Acholiland...' are now crying foul about the lost manhood of their husbands. A close friend of mine, Mr Gabriel Oryema was home to his village where he was hosted well by his relatives. Later on, when he was about to go back to Kampala, six of his sisters-in-law told him that they had a problem to present before him. He obliged and his sisters-in-law informed him that their husbands were impotent what should they do? The culprit was stated to be spirits in the sachets. Their husbands enjoyed to the extreme certain types of spirits in sachets. This has caused Mr Gabriel Oryema's brothers to become impotent.

Mr Gabriel Oryema's told me that he looked at his young sisters-in-law and cried. What else could he do? When he narrated to me the ordeals of his young sister-in-law, I shed tears too in sympathy! I shed tears especially about the death of such homes now in '...Acholiland...' Some women in '...Acholiland...' who are happily married are now thinking about walking out of their marriages because of a problem that has been created by alcoholism. Others are just suffering silently whenever this sort of thing happened in the happy marriages.

k. Disconnects

We have suffered and we shall continue to suffer because we shun unity among ourselves. We divide ourselves on trivial matters along religious lines, political party lines, and along Kitgum/Gulu demarcations or descriptions, at the expense of peace, security, and harmony we should enjoy. One Acholi politician told me during the UNLF era that Uganda will not stabilise unless we Acholi are united because it is the division among Acholi that encourages instability in Uganda. The onus is therefore upon us to unite so that we may live in peace and security and harmony in Uganda.

Flagposts:

1.

Save Uganda Movement – Special Forces deployed during the 1978/1978 Liberation War against Idi Amin-Dada

	Name	Original Career	District of Origin	Deployment
1	Kenneth Kaunda Banya[232]	Airforce Cadet Pilot	Kitgum	Infiltration
2	Henry Oluoch	Airforce Cadet Pilot	Gulu	Frontline
3	Andre Loka	Police	Amuru	Frontline
4	Julius Oketta[233]	Police	Amuru	Infiltration
5	Damiano Ochieng	Soldier	Amuru	Frontline
6	Thomas Oringa	Soldier	Amuru	Infiltration
7	Tonny Lanek	Soldier	Kitgum	Infiltration
8	Paul Opobo Oryema[234]	Teacher	Amuru	Infiltration
9	John Lacere[235]	Peasant	Lamwo	Infiltration
10	Fred Otim	Student	Gulu	Infiltration

---

[232] Built the Kitgum Militia (KiMi), which played other key roles shaping the post-Idi Amin political direction the country? The KiMi was officially handed over by the Tanzania Peoples Defence Force (TPDF) to then President Mr Godfrey Lukongwa-Binaisa in 1979 as its political Commander in Chief. Later years KK resumed career in the Airforce 1980-1985; then joined the Lords Resistance Army's (LRA) 1986-2007 fight against the NRA-regime. After Juba Peace Process took up the NRA-government Amnesty and retired.

[233] Served in the Uganda National Liberation Army (UNLA) 1979-1986; then served the Uganda Peoples Defence Force (UPDF) 1986-2016 rising to the rank of Major General, at the same time Member of Parliament representing the army. Was recalled by the ancestors in 2016, and now rested in Kitgum.

[234] Author

[235] See Dedication

Save Uganda Movement [SUM]

11	Alfred Banya	Student	Gulu	Infiltration
12	Balaam Ongom	Student	Kitgum	Infiltration
13	Justin Obwoya	Student	Kitgum	Infiltration
14	Richard Nono	Student	Kitgum	Infiltration
15	David Apeche	Student	Amuru	Infiltration (AWOL[236])
16	Augustine Lakony	Worker	Amuru	Infiltration (AWOL[237])
17	Ray Okwir	Student	Lira	Infiltration
18	Tony Otuku	Worker	Lira	Infiltration (AWOL[238])
19	Benjamin Ojok[239]	Civil Servant	Lamwo	Frontline
20	Kosuwa	Student	Paliisa	Infiltration
21	Okello Lalur	Student	Lira	Infiltration
22	Oketch Ojukwu[240]	Student	Abim	Infiltration
23	Vincent Ocaya Gongo	Worker	Amuru	Infiltration
24	Bernard Onen[241]	Student	Amuru	Infiltration
25	John Okumu Samora	Student	Gulu	Frontline
26	Moses Musoke	Student	Wakiso	Infiltration
27	Robert Nsubuga Ntege	Student	Buikwe	Infiltration
28	Deo Magara Patel	Soldier	Mbarara	Infiltration
29	Volman	Teacher	Soroti	Infiltration
30	Diim Mayon	Worker	Sironko	Infiltration

---

[236] Military code for AWOL - Absent Without Official Leave. In these cited cases they completed their training and absented themselves from taking further part in executing their assignments.

[237] See Dedication

[238] See Dedication

[239] See Dedication

[240] See Dedication

[241] Served under Uganda National Liberation Army (UNLA) 1979-1985; then at rank of Colonel in the resistance, took up the role of OAU Military Peace Monitoring following the Juba Peace Process 2007 between Lord's Resistance Army (LRA) and National Resistance Army (NRA)-regime.

31	Francis Malinga	Worker	Mbale	Infiltration
32	Mzee Lombe	Civil Servant	Soroti	Infiltration
33	Gulu[242]	Peasant	Soroti	Infiltration
34	David Kitara[243]	Student	Gulu	Infiltration
35	Charles Oburu[244]	Civil Aviation Flight controller	Tororo	Infiltration
36	Ekwaro Ten-Two	Peasant	Soroti	Infiltration
37	Juventus Opecha-Abiriga	Peasant	Amuria	Infiltration
38	Jenaro Ouma	Mechanic	Amuru	Infiltration
39	Collins Chope	Mechanic	Amuru	Infiltration
40	Jenaro Kibwota Mogi	Peasant	Amuru	Infiltration
41	Hitler Eregu[245]	Police	Soroti	Infiltration
42	Etenga Sixy	Social worker	Soroti	Infiltration
43	Esonyu	Peasant	Soroti	Infiltration
44	Thomas Gidudu	Worker	Mbale	Infiltration
45	Olobo TelAviv	Peasant	Soroti	Infiltration
46	Epechu	Student	Soroti	Infiltration
47	Tony Otto	Mechanic	Amuru	Infiltration
48	Elias Wanyama	Worker	Busia	Infiltration

---

[242] See Dedication
[243] See Dedication
[244] See Dedication
[245] Served the Uganda National Liberation Army (UNLA) 1979-1986 rising to a rank of Captain; then head of the Uganda Peoples Army (UPA) – 1987-2006 which was anti-National Resistance Army insurgency. After defeat of UPA, surrendered to the NRA-government under an amnesty.

2

Map of Uganda – spread/origin of SUM special forces

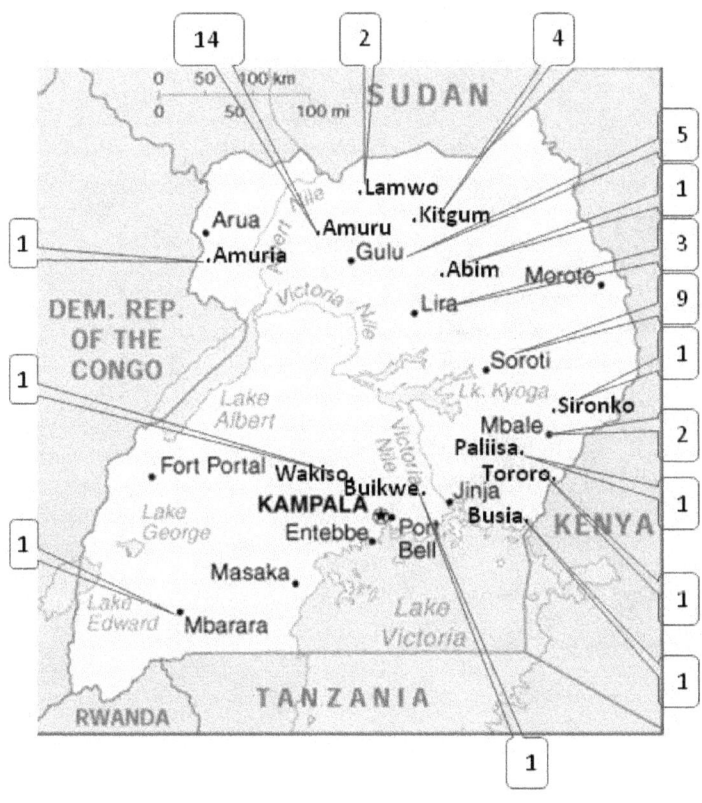

3

SUM Operational Epi-centres 1977-1979

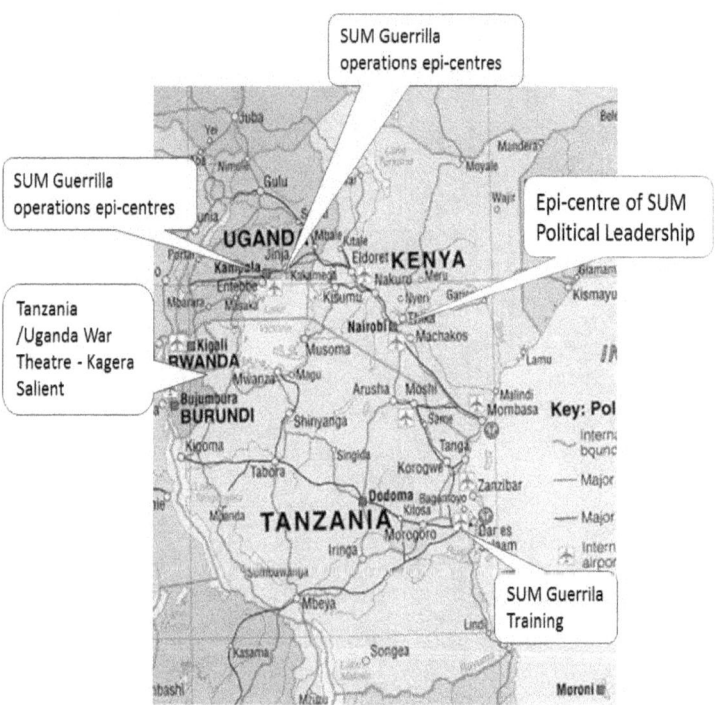

Save Uganda Movement [SUM]

4

SUM Operational Theatres 1978-1979

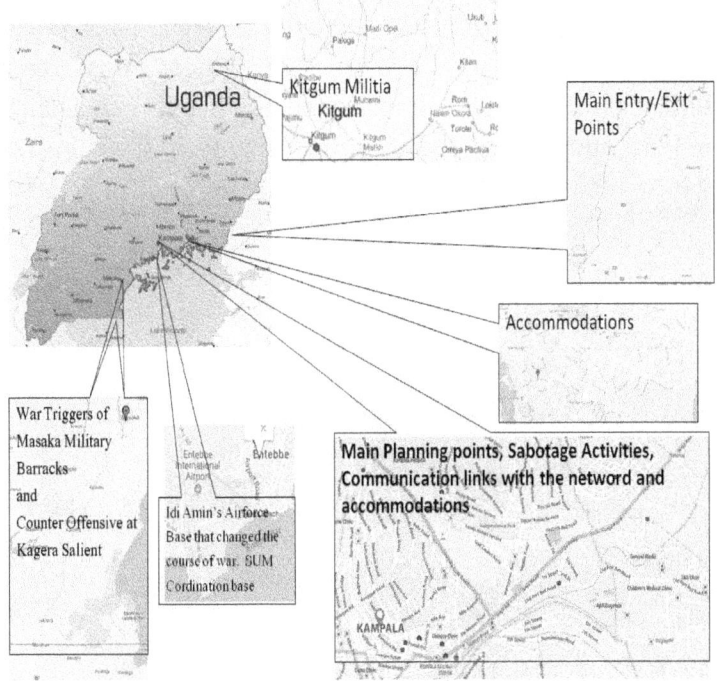

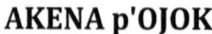

5.

AKENA p'OJOK

Uncelebrated and unmentioned driver/head of Save Uganda Movement (SUM). Later served as Vice Chairman of Uganda National Liberation Front (UNLF)/Minister of Energy, 1978-1980. Member of Parliament and Minister of Power Post and Telecommunication 1980-1985; Imprisoned for 3 years in Luzira Prison 1986-1988 under the Museveni/NRA-regime. Exiled in the United Kingdom 1988- to date of publication.

Epilogue

The author, Mr Paulo Opobo-Oryema (POO), is one of the Save Uganda Movement [SUM] Commanders who after a specialised military training in Tanzania 1977-78, was infiltrated into Uganda to start the 1979 war of liberation against Idi Amin-Dada's murderous regime[246].

POO commanded SUM guerrilla fighters who were based in Kampala and Jinja by carrying out various acts of sabotage of military importance which made it possible for Tanzania Peoples Defence Forces [TPDF] assisted by credible Uganda fighting groups to fight Amin out of power. Let me say it here – POO earned this 'Command leadership' and delivered the liberation project as delegated by the SUM leadership

On the basis of development on the military front once the war started, Uganda politicians in the diaspora were forced into a compromise to form a united front on 26th March 1979, in Moshi, Tanzania for the purpose of replacing a defeated dictatorship. After days of squabbling, the Uganda National Liberation Front [UNLF], a product of 20 Uganda political and military groups was born along with National Consultative Council [NCC] chaired by Mr Edward Rugumayo and the National Executive Committee [NEC] as its supreme organ and respective arms headed by Prof Yusuf Kironde-Lule. Uganda National Liberation Army [UNLA] was proclaimed – with its fighting men already in Uganda.

The group which had met to form the UNLA had very diverse background and political objectives. It was clear from those who attended the hurriedly convened meeting that the option on the table was a military victory but asserting a civilian led-government. This was challenging because of contests and claims of supremacy by the various colleges of interests. All those who assembled had political allegiances and a history or experiences in the body politics

---

[246] Ascended into political governance in 1971 in a military putsch that removed the civilian government under Dr Apollo Milton Obote 1962-1971.

of the country. Individuals or groups knew what they wanted and possibly aimed to impose it, but it was not the time and place, however, was variously tried. It was a sleigh of hand that Tanzania's President Mwalimu[247] Julius Kambarage Nyerere who more than anyone else had the best inside story to be usefully shared and/or may have thought it would be impolitic to share it.

Mwalimu Nyerere's experiences about Uganda and its political dynamics was not only forged as President but from his students days at Makerere University and sharing classrooms elsewhere in Edinburgh University, political and liberation conferences at Africa level; East African level and also Southern Africa platforms in relationship to the universal anti-apartheid struggles.

No doubt that there were newcomers in the assembly who might not have been on Mwalimu Julius Nyerere's political radar but could not have been offering anything new apart from being high achievers in their various fields and passion to remove Idi Amin-Dada regime. Others of course had all these credentials, but their politics and political outlook was ill-at ease with that of Tanzania. Nevertheless, they swallowed their opinion to ride on the back of Tanzania to get rid of Idi Amin-Dada – they made Machiavelli[248] very proud. Their consequent political activities post-Amin was symptomatic of denouncing Tanzania for helping them to rid Uganda of Idi Amin-Dada. Not that they did not try on their own but had no choice as the opportunity had presented itself.

It's against the above that this book is shy to ask Tanzania most serious questions but may be Ugandans in general may start as below:

    a. *"...How did you do it?*
    b. *"...Who were the principle actors, foot soldiers and political operatives from where that Ugandan need to immortalise in*

---

[247] Swahili language for Teacher. Became a reverence title arising from his profession.
[248] Used in the context of the quote: *'...Where the willingness is great, the difficulties cannot be great...'*

> *appreciation of the sacrifices made to rid Uganda of Idi Amin-Dada..."*

There is no doubt this is a challenging story to narrate covering 40 years. It is humanly impossible to address or represent different and differing viewpoints to this end one would urge that:

i. The many and critical principals have been recalled by the ancestors and we should let them rest in peace. There may be hope that their finger-prints variously left somewhere will be prised-off by modern technology for sharing.

ii. Other known principals as variously mentioned here and still variously traversing the planet earth may corroborate or correct the recollection embedded here, may be inadvertently.

iii. The significant others who may have played a key role but were in the penumbra of the writer should not be shy but come forward to, not only ascertain, but provide a different or interesting insight to the ridding of Idi Amin-Dada regime from rulership of Uganda. We shall or will all be the richer.

iv. There may be significant others who disagreed with Tanzania's action or had a differing take on the recollection shared here, they too should share their criticisms as appropriate. The progeny of Uganda should critic this record as we would be the richer for any challenging views, however unpalatable.

May be its fair to mention here that any recollection or narrative organises-in certain things or issues of interest and or organises-out the uninteresting or uncomfortable others. This is a matter of taste. Any passionate reader of this recollection finding oneself in any of these compartments, should feel free to publish own view point(s). This is will deepen the freedom our people ideally yearn for and grow the ideal of 'open society[249]' enriched by ideas and opinions.

Jack & Alecho-oita

---

[249] As advanced by Sir Karl Popper in '...*The Open Society and Its Enemies*...'

Subject Index

1

1900 Buganda Agreement, 71
1962 Constitution, 71, 72, 75, 77, 78
1962 Independence Agreement, 80

2

25th January 1978, 48

9

9th October 1884, 80
9th October 1962, 71

A

Abednego Ongom, 67
Absent Without Official Leave, 182
Acama Oketch, 66
Achelis Ltd, 116
Acholi, 19-23, 25, 26, 104, 105, 124, 149, 150, 152, 154-162, 167-175, 177-179
Acholi War Claimants Association, 178
Acholiland, 142, 149, 150, 156-169, 172-179
Adam and Eve, 149
Addis Ababa, 114, 118
Adoko Nekyon, 73, 140
Adoniya Tiberondwa, 62
Africa Cup of Nations, 37
Africanisation, 82, 83, 84, 85, 112
Afro-Shirazi Party, 84
Air & Seaborne Garrison, 132
Air&Seaborne Battalion, 62
Airforce, 6, 39, 53, 59, 62, 98, 181
AirFrance, 16, 17
Akena Adoko, 74
Akena p'Ojok, 28, 65, 66, 68, 93, 135, 137
Albert Lukwiya, 67, 139
Alfa Romeo, 29, 98
Algeria, 135, 136
Alice Auma Lakwena, 157
Amber House, 102
Amnesty International, 20, 205
Amur District, 14

Amuru, 5, 160, 162, 181, 182, 183, 205
Andrew Adimola, 88
Anglican Bishops, 120
Anglican Church, 123
Angolans, 32, 143
anti-Amin, 7, 62, 92, 93, 97, 130
Anti-Retroviral, 160
Antony Ocaya, 66
Antony Tuhimbise, 204
Apollo Egwau, 67
Apollo Ejou, 29, 36, 41, 43, 86, 138
Apollo Milton Obote, 73, 74, 82, 83, 86, 92
Arab, 57, 108, 110, 126
Archbishop Janani Luwum, 119, 120, 121, 122, 123, 127
Arege, 172
Armoured Personnel Carrier, 114
Army Commander, 73, 76, 82, 111
Army Mutiny, 82
Arusha, 6, 7, 29, 42, 64
Asians, 16, 24, 107, 110, 112, 114, 176
Aswa, 156, 158, 159
Ateker Ejalu, 42, 66, 93, 135
Atlantic World College, 204
Automatic Kalashnikov, 33

B

Bachelor of Arts Social Sciences, 204
Baganda, 70, 71, 77, 78, 79, 80, 203
Balaki Keba Kirya, 74
Bandits, 141
Banyoro, 72
Basil Bataringaya, 75
Bazookas, 33
Ben Msuya, 64
Benedicto Kagimu Mugumba Kiwanuka, 23, 112, 113
Benjamin Coptic Ojok, 4, 68, 182
Benon Ogwal, 123
Berlin Conference, 70
Besigye-Kifefe, 178
Bible, 123
Bill of Rights, 22
Bishop of Kigezi, 88

Save Uganda Movement [SUM]

Bitariho, 145
Black Belt, 136
Bob Odong Nayenda, 134
Britain, 81, 83, 110-112, 114-116, 120
British, 11, 14, 30, 46, 54, 63, 70, 71, 74, 79, 82, 89, 101, 109, 110, 112-115, 128
British American Tobacco, 46, 101
British Broadcasting Corporation, 11, 113
British Colonial Empire, 70
British Governors, 71
British High Commissioner, 74
Buganda crisis, 73
Buganda Government, 70, 71
Buganda Kingdom, 70, 72, 76, 77, 79, 80
Buganda Lukiiko, 75
Bukedi Diocese, 123
Bukoba, 59, 68, 97
Bukoto, 54, 55, 57
Bulange, 76
Bungangaizi, 80
Bungatiro, 159
Bunyoro, 72, 79, 80
Burundi, 103
Bush War, 141
Bushenyi, 93
Busia, 6, 43, 183
Butangira, 156
Butangire, 150
Butebo Station, 64
Butiama, 4
Buyaga and Bugangaizi, 72, 80

C

Canada, 120
Capt. Kaluzi, 30, 32
Capt. Simbeyi, 38
Captain Kaluzi, 143
Cardinal Emmanuel Kiwanuka Nsubuga, 141
Catholics, 15, 24
CAVILAM, 17, 18
Central Executive Committee, 42
Chancellor, 23, 77, 88
Charles Alai, 67
Charles Arube, 91, 125
Charles Oburu, 4, 96, 183

Chief Binyi, 155
Chief Lutaya, 75
Chief Political Commissar, 178
China, 163
Chotta Vuru, 67
Christian Science Monitor, 115
Christianity, 161
Christine Aryemo, 14
Church of Uganda, 19, 120, 127
CK, 100
Coca Plants, 162, 163, 164, 165
Cocaine, 162
Coffee, 102, 107
Coffee Marketing Board, 102
Col. Bolka Bar-Levi, 88
Col. R. Groome, 82
Collins Chope, 54, 57, 183
Colombia, 162, 163
Commission of Inquiry, 74, 75, 108
Commonwealth Games, 111
Conqueror of the British Empire., 63
Constituent Assembly, 89
Constitution, 71, 75, 76, 79, 80, 89, 147, 148
Cooper and Lybrand, 204
Cornelius Ouma, 57, 58
Corporal Muchagga, 30
Corporal Yohama, 39, 40
Corporal Yohanna, 32
coup d'état, 83, 91, 121
coup d'état, 19, 73, 109
Court of St James, 88
Criminal Investigation Department, 57, 58
crocodile, 51, 59

D

Dar es Salaam, 6, 7, 29, 30, 32, 37, 41, 62, 64, , 97, 118
Daudi Ochieng, 73, 74
David Barlow, 129
David Kitara, 4, 96, 105, 183
David Omitta, 53, 59, 98
David Tinyefunza, 159
D-day, 49, 52, 53, 54, 59, 86, 96, 117
Defence Council, 108, 122
Defence Minister, 111
Democratic Party, 3, 23, 67, 75, 113, 137, 140

Democratic Republic of Congo, 5, 74
Denis Hills, 115
Dennis Echwou, 36, 37, 41, 45, 49, 67, 99, 102, 135
Dimie Mayoni, 44
Disco Music System, 155, 156, 161
Donald Steward, 113
Dr Livingstone, 80
Drug Barons, 163

E

East African Airways, 29, 98
East African Community, 38, 42, 99
East African Court of Appeal, 113
East African Distilleries, 172, 176
Economy & Mulengera Newspapers, 79
Edward Mutesa, 72, 73, 74, 76, 77, 80
Edward Rugumayo, 38, 62, 188
Elias Wanyama, 102, 183
Elizabeth Bagaya, 23
Emmanuel B.S. Lumu, 74
Entebbe, 6, 16, 17, 62, 64, 65, 68, 89, 98, 116, 136, 137, 164
Entebbe Airport, 16, 17, 64, 116
Entebbe Raid, 89
Ephraim Kamuntu, 43, 66, 137
Equatorial Brigade, 88
Erinayo Oryema, 19, 74, 120, 122
Erythroxylaceae, 162
ethnic cleansing, 166
Europe, 89

F

Federal Constitution, 78, 79, 81
Fellow of Royal Electronic Engineer, 99
Flagpost, 36, 42-44, 47, 52, 53, 60, 65, 66, 68, 69, 94, 96, 100, 135
Forum for Democratic Change, 178
France, 16, 17, 18, 89, 114, 116, 136
Francis Walugembe, 77
Fredrick Olobo Agwa, 5
French, 16, 17, 19, 49, 204
FRONASA, 3, 61, 69, 92, 93, 95, 114, 128, 129, 131, 140

G

Gabriel Oryema, 179
Gailey and Roberts Company, 73
Garibaldi, 145
Gen. Vasilevskiy, 116
General Certificate of Education, 33
General Election, 137, 139, 140, 141, 142, 203
General Service Unit, 3, 29, 74
George Magezi, 74
Geraldine Auma, 14
German, 94, 116, 157
Ghana's Black Stars, 37
Godwin Sule, 116
goga, 168
Government of Uganda, 75
Governor of Bank of Uganda, 112
Grace Ibingira, 72, 73, 74, 81
Grenades, 33
guerrillas, 16, 43, 51, 92, 93, 99, 112-114, 116, 141, 145
Gulu, 4, 6, 52, 77, 96, 99, 102, 121, 123, 150, 153, 156, 158-160, 162, 164, 165, 179, 181-183
Gurdial Singh, 62

H

Heads of State Summit, 86, 108, 118, 138
Helen Amony, 14
Henry Kissinger, 28
Henry Morton Stanley, 80
Hercules Transport – C130, 113
HIV virus, 159
Holy Father, 126
Holy Spirit Movement, 157
Homosexuality, 160
Honda Civic, 45
House of Bishops, 123
Human Immunodeficiency Virus, 159
Human Rights Commission, 48
Hutu, 17

I

Identity Cards, 43, 56
Idi Amin-Dada, 4-11, 15, 16, 18-24, 26-28, 33-35, 37, 40, 42, 43, 47-49,

51, 53, 55, 56, 58, 59, 62-65, 68, 73-79, 81-134, 138, 143-147, 149, 162, 166, 175, 177, 179, 181, 188-190
Immigration Board, 36
Industrial Court, 48
Inspector General of Police, 19, 55, 74
intelligence unit, 68, 106, 137
Internal Security Organisation, 163
International Baccalaureate, 204
International Conference Centre, 122, 204
International Law, 130
Islam, 172
Israel, 89, 109, 110, 111
Israeli Commandos, 116
Italian, 145

J

Jack Oita Alecho, 5, 29, 53, 59, 67, 98, 99, 101, 102, 139
Jacob Okello-Agwa, 5, 67, 139, 146
James Ntozi, 67
Janani Jakaliya Luwum, 19
Jehovah, 148, 149, 160
Jeroline Apio, 46, 51, 100
Jesus Christ, 121, 122, 123
Jews, 122, 123, 160
Jinja, 6, 9-12, 17, 23, 44-47, 49, 50, 54-56, 58, 63, 67-69, 82, 100, 101, 133, 188
John Barigye, 37
John Malecela, 113
John Okoya, 14, 15, 46, 47, 49, 53, 54, 56, 65, 101-104, 160, 174
John Ruhinda, 134
Joint Refugee Service of Kenya, 25
Joseph Kony, 157, 166, 175, 178, 179
Juba Peace Process, 142, 181, 182
Julius Oketta, 54, 57, 181
Junior Secondary, 15
Justine Ocitti, 25, 43
Juvenal Habyalimana, 17

K

Kabaka, 70, 71, 72, 73, 75, 76, 80
Kabale Diocese, 123
Kabalega, 80
Kabamba Military Training School, 141
Kabwegyere, 61, 66
Kagera, 62, 68, 97, 118
Kagera Salient, 118
Kahangi, 128
Kakooza Mutale, 79
Kakuto, 113
Kakwa, 84, 91, 124
Kalisizo, 113
Kampala, 6, 8, 9, 15, 17, 19, 23, 43, 46, 47, 49, 50, 52, 53, 55-58, 63-69, 77, 91, 97, 99-103, 108, 113, 116, 118-120, 122, 126, 133-135, 138, 139, 141, 166, 179, 188, 204
Kampala City Council, 43, 56
Kampala International Conference Centre, 19
Kanyomozi, 66
Karamagi, 99
Karate, 136
Karl Popper, 190
Karuma Bridge, 10
Kassim Musa Obura, 55
Kenneth Kaunda, 47, 94, 177, 181
Kenneth Kaunda Banya, 47, 94, 181
Kenya, 17, 25, 26, 29, 36, 43, 45, 46, 49, 53, 54, 56, 63, 67, 68, 82, 95, 107, 132, 137, 146
Kenya Police, 50, 137
Key soap, 46
Keyo, 14, 15, 152, 165
Keyo Primary School, 15
Kibuli, 54, 55
Kikos Maalum, 3
Kikosi Maalum, 8, 61, 64, 69, 95, 128, 134
Kikuyu, 54
Kilak, 14, 160, 205
Kilak County, 14
Kilak Hills Comprehensive College, 205
Kilembe Copper Mines, 90
King Faisal, 108
Kings African Rifles, 3, 54, 56, 81, 82, 101, 111, 127, 173
Kinyala Sugar Estate, 90
Kironde-Lule, 9, 64
Kitante Hill Senior Secondary, 16
Kitgum, 3, 6, 8, 47, 52, 94, 104, 130, 176, 179, 181, 182

Kololo Senior Secondary, 16, 19, 49
Kuwait, 109
kwete, 169, 170, 171, 173
Kyabazinga of Busoga, 75
Kyaka Village, 59
Kyotera, 113

L

Labour Party, 115
Lake Victoria, 59, 68
Lamogi, 14, 155, 178
Lamogi clan, 14
Lamogi Rebellion, 14
Lamogi sub-county, 14, 178
Lancaster House, 71, 80
Lance Corporal Mwaipopo, 30
LandRover, 30, 55
Lango, 19-23, 26, 124, 149
Last King of Scotland, 109
Latiina, 169, 170
layibi, 168
Leo Obonyo, 67, 99, 139
Liberation war, 7, 53, 94, 98, 99, 101, 102, 116, 118, 125, 129-132, 145, 146
Libya, 64, 99, 109, 110, 112, 113, 114, 127
Libyan forces, 63
Life President, 91, 116
Light Machine Gun, 33
London, 1, 5, 6, 7, 71, 77, 80, 108
Lord's Resistance Army, 3, 142, 157, 159, 166, 175, 182
Lords Supremo High School, 205
Lorne Owere, 62
Lost Counties, 72, 80
Lt Col Ondoga, 125
Lt. Col. Marjan, 97
Lubiri Palace, 76
Lubowa, 76
Lugazi Sugar Works, 90
Lugogo, 56, 77
Luka Lanek, 47, 67
Lukongwa-Binaisa, 62, 136, 137, 181
Lumumba Avenue, 60
Luo, 14, 15, 25
Lusaka, 7, 37
Lutaaya, 75
Lutheran Church, 41

Luwum Street, 100
Luzira Prison, 187, 205

M

Mabira Forest, 69
Magdalena Apoko, 14
Magendo, 45
Maj. Ogwang, 73
Major Mawiya, 41
Major Olwol, 134
Makarov Pistol, 33, 46, 49, 50, 54, 55, 104, 136
Makerere University, 16, 17, 23, 25, 56, 61, 67, 77, 88, 90, 102, 134, 189, 204
Makindye Military Barracks, 129
Malaba, 138, 142
Malaba Police, 138
Malwa, 58
Manifesto, 139
Map of Uganda, 70, 184
Marine Guards, 115
Martha Honey, 8
Martin Aliker, 88
Martina Anek, 14
Masaka, 6, 62, 77, 92, 118, 119
Maseno Police, 63
Masindi Barracks, 133
Mathias Ngobi, 74
Matovu, 75
Matsiko, 17
Matthew Obado, 48
Mau Mau, 54, 56
Mayanja-Nkangi, 75
Mazzini, 145
Mbale, 45, 182, 183
Mbarara, 6, 62, 92, 93, 118, 119, 182
McKenzie Technical Services, 101
Mehta Senior Secondary School, 204, 205
Member of Parliament, 36, 41, 43, 61, 66, 67, 73, 75, 181, 187
Mengo Hill, 68, 105
Mexico, 162, 163
Michael Ondoga, 23
MiG jet fighters, 96
Military Commission, 3, 39, 41, 66, 69, 132, 133, 136, 140
Military Police, 115

Military Training Team, 111
Minayo Oryema, 14
Minister for Reconstruction and Rehabilitation, 88
Minister of Commerce, 88
Minister of Culture and Community Development, 111
Minister of Defence, 19, 92, 130
Minister of Education, 75, 77
Minister of Finance, 75
Minister of Internal Affairs, 19, 41, 75, 178
Minister of Justice, 73, 74, 75, 76
Minister of Natural Resources, 77
Minister of Planning and economic development, 75
Minister of State for Internal affairs, 82
Minister Without Portfolio, 75
Ministry of Defence, 19, 76
Ministry of Health, 160
Ministry of Planning and Economic Development, 139
Mnazi Moja, 118
Mogadishu Agreement, 92, 93, 113
moko kong'o, 170
Mombasa, 17, 67
Morogoro, 29
Moses Musoke, 43, 50, 182
Moshi, 7, 62, 119, 188
Mozambiquans, 32, 143
Muammar el Qadhafi, 63, 108, 114
Mubende, 69, 132, 133, 135
Mubiru, 112, 116
Munduli, 41
Museveni, 5, 37, 61, 62, 69, 88, 92, 93, 94, 112, 114, 128, 130, 131, 136, 141, 142, 157, 158, 165, 177, 178, 187
Muslims, 24, 37, 120, 172
Mustafa Adrisi, 42, 91, 125
Mutesa-1, 80
Mutukula, 113
Mvule, 62
Mwanga, 80
Mwanza, 68
Mwita-Marwa, 64
myel lyel, 152
Mzee George, 104
Mzee Otoa, 46, 94, 101

N

Nadiope, 75
Nairobi, 3, 6, 7, 25, 28, 29, 42, 43, 45, 46, 47, 50, 59, 61, 63, 65, 66, 74, 88, 97, 98, 99, 101
Nairobi Discussion Group, 3, 7, 61
Nairobi University, 43
Nakasero, 65, 102, 103, 104
Nakawa Estate, 47, 49, 51, 53-56, 58, 65, 66, 103, 104, 113
Nakawa Vocational Institute, 54
Namanga border, 29, 98
Namanve Education Institute, 16
National Consultative Council, 3, 8, 36, 38, 43, 61, 62, 66, 67, 145, 188
National Council of Sports, 111
National Executive Committee, 62, 188
National Insurance Corporation, 99
National Resistance Army, 3, 42, 43, 79, 92, 141, 158, 182, 183
National Resistance Movement, 3, 131
National Teachers College, 16
National Teachers College Kyambogo, 16
National Water and Sewerage Corporation, 44, 101
nationalism, 128
NAZI, 157
Ndaiga, 72
Nile Mansions, 66
Non-Commissioned Officer, 124, 133
Non-Government Organisations, 158
Northern Uganda Diocese, 121
Nsambya Barracks, 105
Nsambya Police, 91, 104, 116
Ntege Lubwama, 77
Ntinda, 54
Nubians, 84
Nwoya, 162, 164, 165
Nyerere, 4, 10, 39, 53, 63, 84, 85, 92, 97, 114, 118, 125, 126, 129, 189

O

Obal, 14
Obote, 23, 29, 35, 58, 61, 62, 67, 69, 72-79, 81-84, 86, 91, 93, 94, 97,

112, 114, 124, 126, 128-132, 135, 138-141, 177, 188, 203
Oboth-Ofumbi, 19, 25, 120, 121, 122
Ocitti Justine, 25
Odoi Chwalle, 67, 99, 102
Ojok Mulozi, 67
Okech Ojukwu, 4
Okello Nokrach, 28
Okello-Okello, 67
Oketch Ojukwu, 54, 66, 104, 105, 182
Okoya, 46, 53, 66, 73, 77, 101, 103, 104
Okumu Samora, 4, 68, 105, 182
Old Kampala Senior Secondary School, 16
Old Portbell Road, 100
Old Testament, 160
O-Level, 69
Olufemi Adefope, 62
Olwoo village, 164
Omaria Lo'Arapai, 66, 133
Omo soap, 46
Omugabe, 37
open society, 190
Organisation of African Unity, 6, 62, 108, 118
Organising Committee, 151, 153, 154
Orly Airport, 17
OTC Bus Park, 57
otogo, 158
Owen Falls Power Station, 9, 11, 45
Oyella, 14
Oyer, 59
Oyite Ojok, 64, 68, 98, 106, 129, 130, 133, 137-142
Oyoo, 44, 101

P

Pabbo, 15, 160
Pagak, 155, 178
Palaro, 156, 158
Palema Parish, 14
Palestine Liberation Organisation, 115
Palestinians, 89
Paul Lubega, 76
Paulo Muwanga, 136, 139, 140
peace and reconciliation, 48
People Newspaper, 42
Permanent Secretary, 19, 74, 88

Peter Otai, 62
Phillip Omondi, 37
phut, 168
Physics/Chemistry/Mathematics, 16
Pontius Pilate, 122
Pope, 126
Popular Front for the Liberation of Uganda, 3, 88
Popular Resistance Army, 141
President of Uganda, 34, 61, 72-75, 77, 80, 86-88, 92, 116, 123, 127, 136, 137, 157
Prime Minister, 23, 61, 72, 73, 75, 76, 82, 83, 115, 177
Princeton University, 205
prophet of Islam, 108
Protestants, 15, 24
Provincial Commissioners, 71
Provincial Governor, 107
Pyela, 178

Q

Quinto Ouma, 45, 49, 67

R

Rachael Ayaa, 56, 100
Radio Mega, 121, 164, 165
Ray Okwir, 42, 182
Relief Education Training Uganda Refugees Now, 88
Republican Constitution, 78, 148
Richard Nixon, 28
Richard Posnett, 11
Robert Mukasa, 88
Robert Serumaga, 88
Rocket Propelled Grenade, 38
Rose Akidi, 14
Rubaga Cathedral, 76
Rutaremara, 17
Rwanda, 3, 17, 103
Rwanda Patriotic Front, 3, 17

S

Sam Bwolya, 144
Sam Kisense, 139
Sam Odaka, 62
Sam Ssebagereka, 112

Sam Walugembe, 59, 98
Samson B. Kiseeka, 76
Samsonite Briefcase, 49
Saudi Arabia, 108, 109
Save Our Soul, 163
Save Uganda Movement, 3-6, 8, 9, 56, 61, 80, 85, 93, 95, 96, 128, 135, 139, 146, 181, 187, 188
Sci-fi, 11
Sebugwawo Amoti, 48
Sega Lodge, 45, 47
Sejusa, 159
Self Loading Rifle, 30, 33
Senior Superintendent of Police, 57
Seraphina Oola, 25
Sergeant Habby, 30
Shaban Opolot, 73, 76, 82
Shafique Arrain, 62
Shauri Moyo, 25
Shield and Spear, 26
Siad Barre, 92
Silas Mpunga, 64
Silver Gidongo, 102, 139
sim sim, 168
Singapore, 86, 138
Sodom and Gomorrah, 160
Soroti, 6, 69, 182, 183
South Africans, 32
South America, 162, 163
South Sudan, 107
Soviet Military, 116
Special Forces, 88, 129, 181
Special Military Force, 68
St Janani Luwum Day, 123
St Lawrence Schools, 205
St Phillips' Cathedral, 121
State Attorney, 99, 102
State Research Bureau, 3, 7, 19, 23, 42, 47, 51, 65, 67, 102-105, 114, 117, 121, 122
Sugar Corporation of Uganda Lugazi, 204
SUM Operational Theatres, 2, 44, 45, 58, 59, 60, 186

T

Tanganyika, 84, 85
Tanganyika African National Union, 84
Tanganyika Army, 84, 85
Tanzania, 3, 4, 7, 8, 13, 23, 28-30, 36, 38-40, 42, 45, 53, 55, 59, 61, 63, 64, 68, 69, 79, 85, 92, 94, 95-101, 106, 112-114, 116-119, 124, 125, 127, 129-131, 135, 139, 143, 181, 188-190
Tanzania Marine, 68
Tanzania Peoples Defence Force, 3, 8, 30, 38, 39, 63, 100, 101, 126, 129, 181
Tanzania Peoples Defence Forces, 8, 61, 85, 98, 116, 118, 124, 188
Tanzanians, 8, 40, 41, 47, 118
Telephone House, 102
Telescopic guns, 136
Teso, 52
The Cranes, 37
Thomas Oringa, 25, 46, 51, 54, 181
Titus Rutaremara, 17
Tom Otuku, 132
Tony Avirgan, 8
Tororo, 62, 112, 120, 132, 183
Total Oil Depot, 54, 55
Trinitrotoluene, 46, 54
Trinity College, 25, 26, 43
Tutsi, 17, 103

U

Uganda, 2-11, 13, 16-27, 29, 33, 34, 36-43, 45-49, 51-85, 87-103, 105-108, 110-121, 123-140, 142, 144, 146-149, 156, 157, 159, 160, 162, 163, 165, 167, 172, 173, 175-178, 180-183, 187-190, 20-205
Uganda Airlines Corporation, 36, 38, 65, 77, 99, 139
Uganda Armed Forces, 19, 20, 21, 22, 56
Uganda Blankets Manufacturers, 100
Uganda Broadcasting Corporation, 100
Uganda Cement Corporation, 89
Uganda Commercial Bank, 57
Uganda Electricity Board, 10, 45, 54
Uganda General Merchandise, 204
Uganda House, 57, 139
Uganda Human Rights Group, 88
Uganda Mass Media, 159
Uganda National Forum, 108

Uganda National Liberation Army, 3, 63, 64, 68, 98, 128, 133, 135, 138, 181, 182, 183, 188, 203
Uganda National Liberation Front, 3, 7, 38, 39, 41, 42, 43, 62, 64-67, 69, 74, 88, 92-94, 107, 112, 119, 128, 137, 139, 187, 188
Uganda National Movement, 3, 7, 37
Uganda National Organisation, 88
Uganda Olympic Committee, 111
Uganda Parliament, 74, 75
Uganda Patriotic Movement, 140
Uganda Peoples Congress, 3, 19, 21, 62, 72, 77, 92, 94, 131, 140, 149
Uganda Peoples Defence Force, 3, 142, 157, 159, 167, 175, 181
Uganda Police, 49, 58, 129, 137
Uganda Posts and Telecommunication, 38, 102
Uganda Protectorate, 70, 71
Uganda Railways Corporation, 38, 42
Uganda Society, 88
Uganda Waragi, 156, 176
Ugandan African Traders Associations, 112
Ugandans, 4, 8, 18, 20-22, 24, 28, 32, 41, 48, 56, 59, 72, 78, 81, 83, 87, 90, 91, 97, 109, 119, 125, 128, 138, 144-147, 149, 161, 163, 166, 176, 189
Union of Soviet Socialist Republics, 111
Unitarist Nationalists, 78
United Kingdom, 5, 72, 76, 115, 187
Unity in Diversity, 78, 147
US Embassy, 115
USA, 28, 116, 205

V

Vanguard Commander of Liberation, 115
Vatican, 126
Very Important Person, 136
VIP Protection, 136, 137

W

Wankoko, 65
Wanume Kibedi, 113
waragi, 107, 172, 173, 175, 176
West Nile, 91, 125
West Nilers, 91
white man's burden, 109, 115
William Ekwaru, 67, 69, 106
William Omaria L'orapai, 41
Wilson Obura, 121, 122, 123
Winnits, 65
World Health Organisation, 176

Y

Yala Police, 50
Yellow Belt, 136
Yona Okoth, 120, 123
Yusuf Kironde-Lule, 9, 62, 64, 65, 88, 188
YWCA, 60, 100

Z

Zambia, 23, 37, 94, 177
Zedekiah Maruru, 39, 41, 66, 69, 133
Zimbabweans, 32, 143

My wandering Profile

&

Author

Paul Opobo Oryema

['Mwalimu' - SUM operational code name]

After the General Election of 10th-11th December 1980, I was deployed at Chief of Defence Force [CDF] office as one of the intelligence officers. I served there for some time and it was not comfortable. I was not being given opportunity to go and attend any officers' course. High ranking military officers' in Uganda National Liberation Army [UNLA] were busy sending their kin and kith for officer training or cadets' course. I was wondering whether there was any merit in that. Well the Baganda have a saying that:

> '...if someone has refused to give you something, then has shown you the way....'

I called it quits and moved to the President's Office. I served as residence security personnel at the Presidents' residence at Kololo, of Dr Apollo Milton Obote. I served there for some time and again I called it quits for the same reason.

I started working with a Uganda parastatal body Uganda General Merchandise (U) Ltd [UGML] in 1981 as a Commercial Officer. The parastatal used to import and sell to the public household goods. But it even operated a Duty-Free shop at International Conference Centre (ICC), Kampala. I worked with UGML up to 1985, and then I got a study leave to go to Makerere University. In 1988, I graduated from Makerere University having attained Hon Bachelor of Arts Social Sciences [BA-SS]. I resumed working with UGML at until it was privatised in 1994. During the privatisation, I remained as a caretaker working with the Auditing Firm Cooper and Lybrand that was liquidating the company.

At the end of the liquidation process of the company in 1977, I went back to my teaching profession and taught various private secondary schools. The first secondary school I worked with was Mehta Senior Secondary School, Lugazi. The school belongs to Sugar Corporation of Uganda Lugazi [SCOUL]. I worked there as a Deputy Headmaster for six years. The success I scored while working with Mehta SSS was that I managed to put the school in International map. This came about in 2002 when my best student in French got an International Scholarship having passed with flying colour his 'O' Level Examination. The conditions for getting the scholarship were two.

> First: The student must pass 'O'-Level Examination with flying colour.

> Second: Must have two International languages in the 'O'-Level Examination one has passed so well.

Our best performing student in the 'O'-Level Examination in 2002 was Mr Antony Tuhimbise. He got Nine Points for eight subjects. He scored Distinction One in Seven of his examination, and Distinction Two in the eight subjects. His two international languages were English and French where he got Distinction One in each of them. He then qualified to be interviewed for the scholarship and in the interview, he emerged the best performer. As a result, he clinched the scholarship. He then went to Atlantic World College in Wales where he did '...*International Baccalaureate*...' after which he proceeded to Princeton University, USA for his degree course. He graduated from Princeton University with BSc and IT. He is now on his way to become a Space Scientist.

From Mehta SSS, I moved to Kilak Hills Comprehensive College, Mpigi, where I worked as Principal of the School, 2005-2006. The Director of the school sold off the school to the Director of St Lawrence Schools for reasons best known to him inadvertently. I then joined Lords Supremo High School, Kabale as Principal - 2007-2008. However, Lords Supremo High School collapsed due to the sabotage of my predecessor. Thereafter, I went back to Lugazi, and later decided to go home to Amuru District in North of Uganda.

I was arrested by the NRA-military intelligence operatives and spent some extended time in Luzira Prison for unstated reasons. Later after a series of court appearances, then was a cursory mention in court of having committed '...*treason*...' Somewhat and at some point, was released and went back home to live in Amuru. From an unquotable source, I am told that my release was due to the Amnesty International (AI) intervention. Anyway, my thanks go to All.

Paul Opobo Oryema

www.ingramcontent.com/pod-product-compliance
Lightning Source LLC
Chambersburg PA
CBHW070146100426
42743CB00013B/2833